MW01672594

SPANISH COOKBOOK

Made Simple, at Home

The Complete Guide Around Spain to the Discovery of the Tastiest Traditional Recipes Such as Homemade Tapas, Paella, Gazpacho, and Much More

Chef MARINO

TABLE OF CONTENTS

Origins of Spanish Cuisine

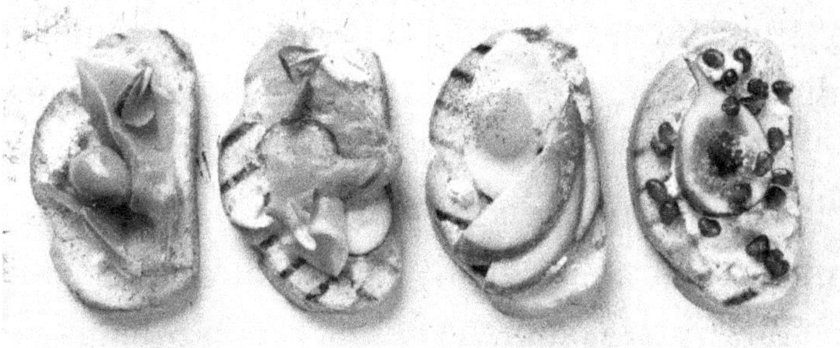

A great past of tradition and gastronomic culture, a sparkling present of innovation and projection into the future. Between tapas and texturas, between the foreign influences that have helped to lay the foundations of traditional cuisine and Ferran Adria's new cuisine, there is no doubt that one of the most interesting European countries, from the point of view of evolution at the table, is Spain.

Like every country overlooking the Mediterranean, over the centuries the local cuisine has been influenced by the Greek one, especially through contact with the Roman civilization, and later the Arabic one; not to mention the very close ties that Spain has had with the countries of the new world: it is precisely in the Iberian peninsula thata bridge has been created, which has allowed the passage of products such as coffee, cocoa, tomatoes, potatoes, from America to Europe. The evolution of gastronomy has been structured on exceptional raw materials, from olive trees "exported" by the Romans to products unknown in the old continent that the conquistadors brought from their travels across the Atlantic; to which we can add the richness of fish products of the Iberian peninsula, the climate favourable to the cultivation of fruit and vegetables, the mountainous reliefs and the traditions of the hinterland that have privileged meat-based food. With similar assumptions, the result was a culinary art in continuous experimentation, which then led to the nuevacocina, and finally to El Bulli, perhaps the most famous restaurant in the world, run by what is called "el mejorcocinero", Ferran Adria. The spearhead of the school of molecular gastronomy, which in every country, including Spain, finds fervent enthusiasts as well as fierce detractors; but which, beyond positive or negative criticism, "traditionalist" or "innovative" positions, was undoubtedly the chef who, more than anyone else, was able to draw unprecedented media and global attention to his work in the history of catering and the evolution of gastronomy.

In order to analyse Spanish culinary traditions in the best way possible, it is good to start from the observation of the territory, which is vast and heterogeneous: as in the case of Italy and Greece, one can also speak of Mediterranean cuisine in the case of Spain, but bearing in mind that in such a vast region, which has both vast coastlines and important mountain ranges, which is affected by centuries of colonization, especially in America, of a vast hinterland, to speak of "a" traditional cuisine would be reductive. Spain has more than one soul, even at the table; and if dishes like tapas or paella are known all-over the world, this does not mean that they exhaust the richness of the national recipe book, nor that they are able to fully define its thickness. The coastal, Atlantic and Mediterranean regions naturally have a cuisine in which fish, seafood and shellfish dishes stand out. They range from shrimps to tuna, lobsters to scallops. In the north there is an important cheese making tradition, which even if it does not put Spain at the level of France or Italy for cheese production, it still offers an abundant production. If the valleys allow the cultivation of fruit and vegetables, especially in the areas, as in the south, where the climate is milder, inland and mountainous reliefs are the fulcrum of sheep farming and meat dishes. When we talk about red meat in Spain we mainly talk about game and pigs: the products that come from certain pig farms are highly prized and internationally famous. The southern part of the country is the one that has been most influenced by Arab culture and offers a greater variety not only of citrus fruits and rice dishes, but also of spices. As for tapas, now considered a national dish, they are largely native to Andalusia, as is another famous dish, gazpacho. The Canary Islands have gastronomic traditions that differ in part from the rest of the country; among the peculiarities, mojos, spicy sauces.

Taking up the subject of typical dishes, it is complex to select representative recipes in such a gastronomic variety, but there is no doubt that some specialities recall the idea of Spanish cuisine all-over the world. Starting with tapas, cold or hot hors d'oeuvres (pinchos in some northern regions);

although it would be more correct to speak of aperitifs, since real hors d'oeuvres are called entremésas. The custom is to eat several of them by moving from place to place (ir de tapas), and considering the vast choice there is no risk of getting bored: they range from meatballs to bread with garlic sauce, from squid rings to olives, to tortillas, which can be served as an appetizer or second course. A product really appreciated by gourmets all-over the world is the Spanish ham, jamòn, of the Pata Negra pig breed. The best hams reach very high prices, but justified by the pigs' diet, left free to eat even only excellent acorns, from the curing, from the processing. Another popular recipe is gazpacho, a cold soup of raw vegetables, usually tomatoes, peppers and cucumbers, but there are dozens of variations, mixed together and served with softened stale bread. But in general when people say Spain, paella comes to mind, a unique dish made with rice, meat, fish or vegetables, which takes its name from the pan in which it is cooked. The original recipe, from Valencia, includes rice, oil, saffron, meat and vegetables; but there are as many variations as the ingredients with which it can be seasoned. Finally, Spain also boasts an excellent oenological tradition, ranging from the wines of Navarre or Jerez to the sparkling wines of Catalonia and Sherry. There are many desserts, of which perhaps the most famous, abroad, is the excellent Catalan cream.

Spanish-Style Cuisine

Famous all-over the world for its traditional dishes, such as paella, gazpacho and Catalan cream, it has the merit of being the first to introduce some ingredients from the Americas, such as tomato, potato, corn or cocoa.Spanish gastronomy enjoys worldwide fame and some of its typical dishes are widespread.It is a very varied cuisine, which includes dishes and recipes from different geographical areas and cultures. In fact, one cannot speak of a real national cuisine, but of regional cuisines with very different characteristics.

Many ingredients of Mediterranean cuisine have been introduced to Europe through Spain, especially those from the Americas. So, today Spanish recipes cannot miss potatoes, tomatoes, peppers and beans.

The essential ingredient for cooking dishes is olive oil (Spain produces 44% of the world's olives), although butter is very important in the cuisine of the north of the country.

A good part of Spanish cuisine has its roots in the Jewish and Moorish traditions, which have had a strong influence in the country for many centuries. In fact, some of these recipes are still prepared today.However, pork is a widespread ingredient and for centuries consuming this type of meat has also taken on a symbolic value, that of reaffirming one's Christianity.

The cuisine of the regions facing the sea (Catalonia, ComunidadValenciana, Andalusia, Canary Islands) also includes meat and fish dishes, including mussels, scallops, lobsters, octopus, anchovies and tuna, and is more varied than that of the more inland areas, based essentially on meat and legumes.

Here are some dishes that you can't miss if you visit Spain:

- Cocido madrileño: even if it is not a properly light and summery dish, it is a real institution in Madrid, a very ancient dish still strongly rooted in the daily life of modern Madrid. It is a stew made with chickpeas, various types of meat, sausages and vegetables cooked for a long time over low heat.

- Gazpacho: is a traditional cold soup, which can be found in various regions of Spain, such as Extremadura, Andalusia and Castile-La Mancha. The most popular is the Andalusian one, which is prepared with tomatoes, peppers and garlic. Suitable to be eaten during hot summer days, besides being healthy it is also very good.

- Octopus a feira: this typical Galician octopus dish is served on a wooden plate, with a little coarse salt, paprika and olive oil.

- Fabada: If you want to regain your strength, this Asturian dish is for you. It contains white beans cooked in a soup with black pudding, sausage, bacon and pork shoulder.

- Paella: perhaps the most famous Spanish recipe in the world. There are several versions, although the authentic one is the Valencian paella, prepared with Valencia rice, chicken, rabbit, snails, white beans, soft beans, green beans, garlic, tomatoes, paprika and saffron.

- Lamb with chilindrón: in Navarre, lamb is prepared with a sauce made from fresh, dried peppers, onions and tomatoes.

- Jerte-style fried tench: a typical Extremadura dish in which Iberian ham is fried together with garlic in the frying oil of tench.

- Potato tortilla: onion, eggs and potatoes are the ingredients of the Spanish dish par excellence, unfailing in any place.

- Cod with pil-pil: in the Basque Country it is prepared using few ingredients, but all the chef's skill in treating the fish's moods is indispensable to obtain a delicious sauce.

- Roast suckling lamb: this delicacy, typical of the gastronomy of Castile and Leon, is traditionally cooked in a wood-fired oven in a terracotta pot.

- Churros: these inevitable fried sticks are eaten at breakfast or as a snack, of course, accompanied by hot chocolate and sprinkled with stevia icing. They say it is one of King Juan Carlos' favourite desserts.

- Tocino de cielo: the most beloved and widespread Andalusian dessert, a little reminiscent of crème caramel. It seems to have been invented in 1324 by the nuns of the convent of Jerez de la Frontera.

- Torta de Santiago: delicious almond-flavoured cake decorated with the cross of Santiago, it is the main dessert of Galician cuisine and a classic in the suitcase of the pilgrims who complete the Pilgrim's Way to Santiago.

TAPAS

Olive and Anchovy Bites Tapas

In Spain, the motto is “eat when you drink, drink when you eat” – and tapasseem to have been invented for just this. Tapas are finger food, a choice ofdelicious morsels to tempt the drinker to have another glass and with it anothertapas dish. They range from simple dishes of olives and nuts to marinated fishand titbits on skewers.

Sweet and Salty Vegetable Crisps

The Spanish love colourful snacks. Try these brightly coloured vegetable
crisps, which make an appealing alternative to the usual potato crisps. Servethem with a bowl of creamy, garlicky aioli, and use the crisps to scoop it up.

SERVES 4

1 smallfresh beetroot (beet)
caster (superfine) sugar andfine salt,for sprinkling
olive oil,for frying
coarse sea salt, to serve

Directions

1 Peel the beetroot and, using a mandolin or a vegetable peeler, cut it into verythin slices.
2 Lay the slices on kitchen paper and sprinkle them with sugar and fine salt.
3 Heat 5cm/2in oil in a deep pan until a cube of bread turns golden in 1 minute.Cook the slices in batches, until they float to the surface and turn golden at theedge. Drain on kitchen paper and sprinkle with sea salt once they are cool.

Nutritional information per portion: Energy 155kcal/639kJ; Protein 0.3g; Carbohydrate 1.4g, of whichsugars 1.3g; Fat 6.5g, of which saturates 2.4g; Cholesterol 0mg; Calcium 4mg; Fibre 0.4g; Sodium 13mg.

Olive and Anchovy Bites

These little melt-in-the-mouth morsels are made from two ingredients that areforever associated with tapas – olives and anchovies. The reason for this is thatboth contain salt, which helps to stimulate thirst and therefore drinking.

MAKES 40–45

115g/4oz/1 cup plain (all-purpose) flour
115g/4oz/1/2 cup chilled butter, diced
115g/4oz/1 cup finely grated Manchego, mature (sharp) Cheddar or
Gruyère cheese
50g/2oz can anchovy fillets in oil, drained and roughly chopped
50g/2oz/1/2 cup pitted black olives, roughly chopped
2.5ml/1/2 tsp cayenne pepper
sea salt, to serve (optional)

Directions

1 Place the flour, butter, cheese, anchovies, olives and cayenne pepper in a foodprocessor and pulse until the mixture forms a firm dough.
2 Wrap the dough loosely in clear film (plastic wrap). Chill in the refrigerator for20 minutes.
3 Preheat the oven to 200°C/400°F/Gas 6. Remove the dough from the

refrigerator, then roll it out thinly on a lightly floured surface.

4 Cut the dough into 5cm/2in wide strips, then cut across each strip in alternatedirections, to make triangles. Transfer the triangles to baking sheets and bake for8–10 minutes until golden. Cool on a wire rack. Sprinkle with sea salt, if desired.

Nutritional information per anchovy bite: Energy 42kcal/173kJ; Protein 1.2g; Carbohydrate 2g, of whichsugars 0.1g; Fat 3.2g, of which saturates 1.9g; Cholesterol 9mg; Calcium 27mg; Fibre 0.1g; Sodium 103mg.

Pimiento Tartlets

Known as tartalitas de pimiento in Spain, these pretty little tartlets are filledwith strips of roasted sweet peppers and a deliciously creamy custard. They areperfect to serve with drinks.

SERVES 4

1 red (bell) pepper
1 yellow (bell) pepper
175g/6oz/11/2 cups plain (all-purpose) flour
75g/3oz/6 tbsp chilled butter, diced
30–45ml/2–3 tbsp cold water
60ml/4 tbsp double (heavy) cream
1 egg
15ml/1 tbsp freshly grated Parmesan cheese
salt and ground black pepper

Directions

1 Preheat the oven to 200°C/400°F/Gas 6, and heat the grill (broiler). Place the peppers on a baking sheet and grill (broil) the peppers for 10 minutes, turning occasionally until blackened. Cover and leave for 5 minutes. Peel off skin, discard the seeds and cut the flesh into strips.

2 Sift the flour and a pinch of salt into a bowl. Rub in the butter until the mixture resembles fine

breadcrumbs. Stir in enough water to make a firm, but not sticky, dough.

3 Roll the dough out thinly on a lightly floured surface and line 12 individual moulds or a 12-hole tartlet tin (muffin pan). Prick the bases with a fork and fill the cases with crumpled foil. Bake for 10 minutes. Remove the foil from the pastry cases and divide the pepper strips among the pastry cases.

4 Whisk the cream and egg in a bowl. Season and pour over the peppers.

Sprinkle each tartlet with cheese and bake for 15–20 minutes until firm. Cool for2 minutes, then transfer to a wire rack. Serve the tartlets warm or cold.

Nutritional information per portion: Energy 427kcal/1778kJ; Protein 8.4g; Carbohydrate 40g, of which sugars 6.4g; Fat 27g, of which saturates 16.1g; Cholesterol 112mg; Calcium 131mg; Fibre 2.8g; Sodium 180mg.

Spinach Empanadillas

Little pies are part of the Moorish tradition in Spain. The Arabs introduced spinach to Europe and pine nuts and raisins are typical Arab ingredients. In Spain, the dough is sold ready-cut in rounds.

MAKES 20

25g/1oz/1/4 cup raisins
25ml/11/2 tbsp olive oil
450g/1lb fresh spinach leaves, washed, drained and chopped
6 canned anchovies, drained and chopped
2 garlic cloves, finely chopped
25g/1oz/1/4 cup pine nuts, roughly chopped
350g/12oz puff pastry
1 egg, beaten
salt and ground black pepper

Directions

1 To make the filling, soak the raisins in warm water for 10 minutes. Drain well, then chop them roughly.
2 Heat the olive oil in a pan, add the spinach, stir, then cover and cook over allow heat for about 2 minutes until the spinach starts to wilt. Remove the lid, turnup the heat and cook until any liquid has evaporated.

3 Add the anchovies, garlic and seasoning to the spinach and cook, stirring, for 1minute. Remove from the heat. Stir in the raisins and pine nuts. Cool.
4 Meanwhile, preheat the oven to 180°C/350°F/Gas 4. Roll out the pastry on alightly floured surface to a 3mm/1/8in thickness.
5 Using a 7.5cm/3in pastry cutter, cut the pastry into 20 rounds. Place about10ml/2 tsp filling in the middle of each round, then brush the edges with a little water. Bring up the sides of the pastry and seal well. Press the edges together with the back of a fork. Brush with egg.
6 Place the pies on a greased baking sheet and bake for 15 minutes, or until puffed up and golden. Transfer the pies to a wire rack to cool. Serve warm.

Nutritional information per empanadilla: Energy 100kcal/416kJ; Protein 2.4g; Carbohydrate 8.1g, of which sugars 1.8g; Fat 6.8g, of which saturates 0.3g; Cholesterol 10mg; Calcium 62mg; Fibre 0.8g; Sodium 98mg.

Tapas of Almonds, Olives and Cheese

Almonds and olives used to be served free in all tapas bars, and still are in some. They are the perfect nibble for pre-dinner drinks. Manchego cheese in oil is now a delicious Spanish export, although you can easily marinate the cheese yourself.

SERVES 6–8

FOR THE MARINATED OLIVES

2.5ml/1/2 tsp coriander seeds

2.5ml/1/2 tsp fennel seeds

2 garlic cloves, crushed

5ml/1tsp chopped fresh rosemary

10ml/2 tsp chopped fresh parsley

15ml/1 tbsp sherry vinegar

30ml/2 tbsp olive oil

115g/4oz/2/3 cup black olives

115g/4oz/2/3 cup green olives

FOR THE MARINATED CHEESE

150g/5oz Manchego or other firm cheese

90ml/6 tbsp olive oil

15ml/1 tbsp white wine vinegar

5ml/1 tsp black peppercorns

1 garlic clove, sliced

fresh thyme or tarragon sprigs

fresh flat leaf parsley or tarragon sprigs, to garnish (optional)

FOR THE SALTED ALMONDS
1.5ml/1/4 tsp cayenne pepper
30ml/2 tbsp sea salt, plus extra for sprinkling (optional)
25g/1oz/2 tbsp butter
60ml/4 tbsp olive oil
200g/7oz/13/4 cups blanched almonds

Directions

1 To make the marinated olives, crush the coriander and fennel seeds in a mortar with a pestle. Work in the garlic, then add the rosemary, parsley, vinegar and olive oil. Put the olives in a small bowl and pour over the marinade. Cover with clear film (plastic wrap) and chill for up to 1 week.

2 To make the marinated cheese, cut the cheese into bitesize pieces, removing any hard rind, and put in a small bowl. Combine the oil, vinegar, pepper corns, garlic and thyme or tarragon and pour over the cheese. Cover with clear film and chill for up to 3 days.

3 To make the salted almonds, combine the cayenne pepper and salt in a bowl. Melt the butter with the oil in a frying pan. Add the almonds and fry them, stirring, for 5 minutes, or until golden. Add the almonds to the salt mixture and toss until the almonds are coated. Leave to cool, then store in an airtight container for up to 1 week.

4 To serve, arrange the almonds, olives and cheese in three separate small, shallow dishes. Garnish the cheese with fresh herbs if you like and sprinkle the almonds with a little more salt, to taste.

Nutritional information per portion: Energy 432kcal/1784kJ; Protein 10.3g; Carbohydrate 1.8g, of which sugars 1.1g; Fat 42.3g, of which saturates 9.7g; Cholesterol 25mg; Calcium 217mg; Fibre 2.7g; Sodium 805mg.

Marinated Anchovies

This is one of the simplest ways to prepare these tiny fish because it requires no cooking. Marinating is particularly associated with anchovies, which tend to lose their freshness quickly.

SERVES 4

225g/8oz fresh anchovies, heads and tails removed, and split open along the belly
juice of 3 lemons
30ml/2 tbsp extra virgin olive oil
2 garlic cloves, finely chopped
15ml/1 tbsp chopped fresh parsley
flaked sea salt

Directions

1 Place the anchovies on a clean work surface and turn them on to their bellies, then press them down with your thumb. 2 Using the tip of a small, sharp knife, carefully remove the backbones from the flattened fish, and then arrange the anchovies skin side down in a single layer on a large plate.
3 Squeeze two-thirds of the lemon juice over the fish and sprinkle them with the salt. Cover and leave to stand for up to 24 hours, basting occasionally with the

juices, until the flesh is white and no longer translucent.

4 Transfer the anchovies to a serving plate and drizzle with the olive oil and the remaining lemon juice. Sprinkle the fish with the chopped garlic and parsley, then cover with clear film (plastic wrap) and chill until ready to serve.

Nutritional information per portion: Energy 144kcal/597kJ; Protein 11.7g; Carbohydrate 0.1g, of which sugars 0.1g; Fat 10.7g, of which saturates 2.3g; Cholesterol 0mg; Calcium 55mg; Fibre 0.2g; Sodium 69mg.

Flash-Fried Squid with Paprika and Garlic

This dish can be served as tapas with a fino or manzanilla sherry.
Alternatively, serve the squid on a bed of salad leaves, accompanied by bread, for a substantial first course to serve four.

SERVES 6–8

500g/11/4lb very small squid, cleaned
90ml/6 tbsp olive oil
1 fresh red chilli, seeded and finely chopped
10ml/2 tsp Spanish mild smoked paprika
30ml/2 tbsp plain (all-purpose) flour
2 garlic cloves, finely chopped
15ml/1 tbsp sherry vinegar
5ml/1 tsp grated lemon rind
30–45ml/2–3 tbsp finely chopped fresh parsley
salt and ground black pepper

Directions

1 Cut the squid body sacs into rings and cut the tentacles into pieces.
2 Place the squid in a bowl. Mix 30ml/2 tbsp of the olive oil with half the chilli, the paprika, salt and pepper, and pour over the squid. Cover with clear film(plastic wrap), then place in the refrigerator and leave to marinate for 2–4 hours.

3 Toss the squid in the flour and divide it into two batches. Heat the remaining oil in a wok or deep frying pan over a high heat until very hot. Add the first batch of squid and quickly stir-fry for 1–2 minutes, or until it becomes opaque and the tentacles curl.

4 Add half the garlic. Stir, then turn out into a bowl. Repeat with the second batch of squid, adding more oil if needed.

5 Sprinkle with the vinegar, lemon rind, remaining chilli and parsley. Season and serve either hot or cool.

Nutritional information per portion: Energy 139kcal/580kJ; Protein 10.1g; Carbohydrate 3.8g, of which sugars 0.1g; Fat 9.4g, of which saturates 1.4g; Cholesterol 141mg; Calcium 21mg; Fibre 0.3g; Sodium70mg.

Sizzling Prawns

Garlic prawns are hugely popular in Spain, both with and without the addition of chilli. They are normally cooked in small, individual earthenware casseroles, which stand on a traditional thick iron plate – la plancha. A frying pan will produce the same result.

SERVES 4

1–2 dried chillies (to taste)
60ml/4 tbsp olive oil
3 garlic cloves, finely chopped
16 large raw prawns (shrimp), in the shell
French bread, to serve

Directions

1 Split the chillies lengthways and discard the seeds. It is best to do this with a knife and fork, because the inner membranes contain a lot of capsaicin, which can be irritating to the eyes, nose and mouth.
2 Heat the oil in a large frying pan and stir-fry the garlic and chilli for 1 minute, until the garlic begins to turn brown.
3 Add the whole prawns and stir-fry for 3–4 minutes, coating them well with the flavoured oil.
4 Remove from the heat and divide the prawns among four dishes. Spoon over the flavoured oil and serve immediately, with French bread. (Remember to

provide a plate for the heads and shells, plus plenty of napkins for messy fingers)

Nutritional information per portion: Energy 147kcal/607kJ; Protein 11g; Carbohydrate 0g, of which sugars0g; Fat 11.4g, of which saturates 1.6g; Cholesterol 122mg; Calcium 50mg; Fibre 0g; Sodium 119mg.

King Prawns in Crispy Batter

A huge range of prawns are eaten in Spain, each with its appropriate cooking method. Langostinos are deep-water prawns, often with tiger stripes, and can be among the biggest. The best way to enjoy them is dipped in a simple batter and deep-fried.

SERVES 4

120ml/4fl oz/1/2 cup water
1 large (US extra large) egg
115g/4oz/1 cup plain (all-purpose) flour
5ml/1 tsp cayenne pepper
12 raw king prawns (jumbo shrimp), in the shell
vegetable oil, for deep-frying
flat leaf parsley, to garnish
lemon wedges, to serve (optional)

Directions

1 In a large bowl, whisk together the water and the egg. Whisk in the flour and cayenne pepper until the mixture is smooth.

2 Peel the prawns, leaving just the tails intact. Using a sharp knife, make a shallow cut down the back of each prawn.

3 Using the tip of the knife, carefully pull out and discard the dark intestinal tract.

4 Heat the oil in a large pan or deep-fryer, until a cube of bread dropped into the oil browns in 1 minute.
5 Holding the prawns by their tails, dip them into the batter, one at a time, shaking off any excess. Carefully drop each prawn into the oil and fry for 2–3minutes until crisp and golden. Drain on kitchen paper, garnish with parsley and serve with lemon wedges, if you like.

Nutritional information per portion: Energy 253kcal/1061kJ; Protein 13.1g; Carbohydrate 22.4g, of which sugars 0.4g; Fat 13.1g, of which saturates 1.8g; Cholesterol 145mg; Calcium 87mg; Fibre 0.9g; Sodium 113mg.

Butterflied Prawns in Chocolate Sauce

There is a long tradition in Spain, which originates in Mexico, of cookingsavoury food – even shellfish – with chocolate. This dish is known aslangostinosen chocolate in Spanish.

SERVES 4

8 large raw prawns (shrimp), in the shell
15ml/1 tbsp seasoned plain (all-purpose) flour
15ml/1 tbsp pale dry sherry
juice of 1 large orange
15g/1/2oz dark (bittersweet) chocolate, chopped
30ml/2 tbsp olive oil
2 garlic cloves, finely chopped
2.5cm/1in piece fresh root ginger, finely chopped
1 small dried chilli, seeded and chopped
salt and ground black pepper

Directions

1 Peel the prawns, leaving just the tail sections intact. Make a shallow cut down the back of each one and pull out and discard the dark tract.

2 Turn the prawns over so that the undersides are uppermost, and then cut them open from tail to top, almost to the central back line.

3 Press the prawns down firmly to flatten them. Coat with the flour and set aside. Gently heat the sherry and

orange juice in a pan. When warm, remove from the heat and stir in the chopped chocolate until melted.

4 Heat the oil in a large frying pan. Add the chopped garlic, ginger and chilli and cook for 2 minutes until golden. Remove with a slotted spoon and reserve. Add the prawns, cut side down, and cook for 2–3 minutes until golden brown with pink edges. Turn them and cook for a further 2 minutes.

5 Return the garlic mixture to the pan and add the chocolate sauce. Cook for 1minute, turning the prawns to coat them in the sauce. Season and serve hot.

Nutritional information per portion: Energy 125kcal/520kJ; Protein 8.5g; Carbohydrate 6.5g, of which sugars 3.6g; Fat 6.9g, of which saturates 1.5g; Cholesterol 88mg; Calcium 44mg; Fibre 0.2g; Sodium 88mg.

Spiced Clams

Spanish clams, especially in the north, are much larger than clams found elsewhere, and have more succulent bodies. This modern recipe uses Arab spicing to make a hot dip or sauce. Serve with plenty of fresh bread to mop up the delicious juices.

SERVES 3–4

1 small onion, finely chopped
1 celery stick, sliced
2 garlic cloves, finely chopped
2.5cm/1in piece fresh root ginger, grated
30ml/2 tbsp olive oil
1.5ml/1/4 tsp chilli powder
5ml/1 tsp ground turmeric
30ml/2 tbsp chopped fresh parsley
500g/11/4lb small clams, in the shell
30ml/2 tbsp dry white wine
salt and ground black pepper
celery leaves, to garnish
fresh bread, to serve

Directions

1 Place the onion, celery, garlic and ginger in a large pan, add the olive oil,spices and chopped parsley and stir-fry for about 5 minutes. Add the clams to the pan

and cook for 2 minutes. 2 Add the wine, then cover and cook gently for 2–3 minutes, shaking the pan occasionally. Season. Discard any clams whose shells remain closed, then serve, garnished with the celery leaves.

COOK'S TIP

There are many varieties of clam. The almejafina (carpet shell clam) is perfect for this dish. Before cooking, check that all the shells are closed, and discard any that do not close when tapped. Discard any clams that do not open after cooking.

Nutritional information per portion: Energy 92kcal/381kJ; Protein 6.5g; Carbohydrate 2.2g, of which sugars 1.1g; Fat 5.9g, of which saturates 0.9g; Cholesterol 25mg; Calcium 50mg; Fibre 0.7g; Sodium 458mg.

Mussels with a Parsley Crust

The stormy Atlantic coast of Spain produces the best mussels in the world. They grow to an enormous size very quickly, without becoming tough. Here they are grilled with a delicious topping, which helps to stop them becoming overcooked.

SERVES 4

450g/1lb fresh mussels
45ml/3 tbsp water
15ml/1 tbsp melted butter
15ml/1 tbsp olive oil
45ml/3 tbsp freshly grated Parmesan cheese
30ml/2 tbsp chopped fresh parsley
2 garlic cloves, finely chopped
2.5ml/1/2 tsp coarsely ground black pepper
crusty bread, to serve

Directions

1 Scrub the mussels thoroughly, scraping off any barnacles with a round-bladed knife and pulling out the gritty beards. Sharply tap any open mussels and discard any that fail to close or whose shells are broken.

2 Place the mussels in a large pan and add the water. Cover the pan with a lid and steam for about 5 minutes, or until the mussel shells have opened.

3 Drain the mussels well and discard any that remain closed. Carefully snap off the top shell from each mussel, leaving the actual flesh still attached to the bottom shell.

4 Balance the shells upright in a flameproof dish, packing them closely together to make sure that they stay level.

5 Preheat the grill (broiler) to high. Put the melted butter, olive oil, Parmesan cheese, parsley, garlic and black pepper in a small bowl and mix well to combine.

6 Spoon a small amount of the cheese and garlic mixture on top of each mussel and gently press down with the back of the spoon.

7 Grill (broil) the mussels for about 2 minutes, or until they are sizzling and golden. Serve the mussels in their shells, with bread to mop up the juices.

Nutritional information per portion: Energy 110kcal/456kJ; Protein 5.4g; Carbohydrate 0.3g, of which sugars 0.3g; Fat 9.7g, of which saturates 4.7g; Cholesterol 21mg; Calcium 165mg; Fibre 0.6g; Sodium156mg.

Chicken Croquettes

Croquetas are popular tapas fare and there are many variations. This one is based on béchamel sauce, which is perfect for taking on different flavours such as ham or chopped peppers.

SERVES 4

25g/1oz/2 tbsp butter
25g/1oz/1/4 cup plain (all-purpose) flour
150ml/1/4 pint/2/3 cup milk
15ml/1 tbsp olive oil, plus extra for deep-frying
1 boneless chicken breast with skin, diced
1 garlic clove, finely chopped
1 small egg, beaten
50g/2oz/1 cup stale white breadcrumbs
salt and ground black pepper
fresh flat leaf parsley, to garnish
lemon wedges, to serve

Directions

1 Melt the butter in a pan. Add the flour and cook gently, stirring, for 1 minute. Gradually stir in the milk and cook until smooth and thick. Cover and set aside.
2 Heat the oil in a frying pan and fry the diced chicken and garlic together, turning, for 5 minutes.
3 When the chicken is lightly browned and cooked through, put the contents of the frying pan into a food

processor and process until finely chopped. Add the mixture to the sauce and stir to combine. Season to taste, then leave to cool.

4 Once cooled and firm, shape the mixture into eight small sausage shapes. Dip each one in beaten egg, then roll in breadcrumbs to coat.

5 Heat the oil in a pan, until a cube of bread dropped in the oil browns in 1minute. Lower the croquettes into the oil and cook for 4 minutes until crisp and golden, then drain on kitchen paper. Serve with lemon wedges and garnish with parsley.

Nutritional information per portion: Energy 286kcal/1195kJ; Protein 13.9g; Carbohydrate 16.4g, of which sugars 2.2g; Fat 18.9g, of which saturates 5.8g; Cholesterol 89mg; Calcium 80mg; Fibre 0.5g; Sodium 189mg.

Barbecued Mini Ribs

These tasty ribs are known as costillas in Spain. They are delicious cooked on a barbecue or under a hot grill. If you prefer a sweeter flavour, use freshly squeezed orange juice instead of sherry.

SERVES 6–8

1 sheet of pork ribs, about 675g/11/2lb
90ml/6 tbsp sweet oloroso sherry
15ml/1 tbsp tomato purée (paste)
5ml/1 tsp soy sauce
2.5ml/1/2 tsp Tabasco sauce
15ml/1 tbsp light muscovado (brown) sugar
30ml/2 tbsp seasoned plain (all-purpose) flour
coarse sea salt

Directions

1 Separate the ribs, then, using a meat cleaver or heavy knife, cut each rib in half width ways to make about 30 pieces.
2 Mix the sherry, tomato purée, soy sauce, Tabasco and sugar together in a bowl. Stir in 2.5ml/1/2 tsp salt.
3 Put the seasoned flour in a strong plastic bag, then add the ribs and toss to coat. Dip each rib in the sauce. Cook on a hot barbecue or under a hot grill (broiler)for 30–40 minutes, turning occasionally until cooked and a little charred. Sprinkle with salt and serve.

COOK'S TIP

Oloroso sherry has a full body and sweet flavour sometimes reminiscent of port.

Nutritional information per portion: Energy 469kcal/1977kJ; Protein 15g; Carbohydrate 66.7g, of which sugars 3.9g; Fat 16.8g, of which saturates 5.5g; Cholesterol 38mg; Calcium 193mg; Fibre 2.7g; Sodium1146mg.

Buñuelos

The name of these cheese puffs literally means puffball. In Spain, they are usually deep-fried, but baking is easier and gives wonderful results. The dough is made in the same way as French choux pastry, and the buñuelos should be eaten within a few hours of baking.

SERVES 4

50g/2oz/1/4 cup butter, diced
1.5ml/1/4 tsp salt
250ml/8fl oz/1 cup water
115g/4oz/1 cup plain (all-purpose) flour
2 whole eggs, plus 1 yolk
2.5ml/1/2 tsp Dijon mustard
2.5ml/1/2 tsp cayenne pepper
50g/2oz/1/2 cup finely grated Manchego or Cheddar cheese

Directions

1 Preheat the oven to 220°C/425°F/Gas 7. Place the butter and the salt in a pan, then add the water. Bring the liquid to the boil. Meanwhile, sift the flour on to a sheet of baking parchment or greaseproof (waxed) paper.

2 Working quickly, tip the flour into the pan of boiling liquid in one go and stir it in immediately. Beat the mixture vigorously with a wooden spoon until it forms

a thick paste that binds together and leaves the sides of the pan clean. Remove the pan from the heat.

3 Gradually beat the eggs and yolk into the mixture, then add the mustard, cayenne pepper and cheese.

4 Place teaspoonfuls of mixture on a non-stick baking sheet and bake for 10minutes. Reduce the temperature to 180°C/350°F/Gas. Cook for 15 minutes until well browned. Serve hot or cold.

Nutritional information per portion: Energy 296kcal/1235kJ; Protein 9.9g; Carbohydrate 22.5g, of which sugars 0.6g; Fat 18.9g, of which saturates 10.5g; Cholesterol 184mg; Calcium 156mg; Fibre 0.9g; Sodium 223mg.

Chicharrones

The Spanish eat everything that comes from the pig, and even the humble rind goes into making this delicious little salted, piquant snack. This crispy, crunchy pork crackling is the perfect accompaniment for a glass of wine or chilled bottle of lager.

SERVES 4

115g/4oz pork rind
vegetable oil, for frying
paprika and coarse sea salt, for sprinkling

Directions

1 Using a sharp knife, cut the pork rind into strips. There is no need to be too precise, but try to make the strips roughly 1cm/1/2in wide and 2.5cm/1in long.
2 Pour the vegetable oil to a depth of 2.5cm/1in in a deep, heavy frying pan. Heat the oil and check that it has reached the correct temperature by immersing a cube of bread, which should brown in 1 minute.
3 Cook the strips of rind in the oil for 1–2 minutes, until they are puffed up an golden brown. Remove with a slotted spoon and drain on kitchen paper.
4 Sprinkle the chicharrones with paprika and salt to taste. Serve them hot or cold. Although they are at their best 1–2 days after cooking, they will keep reasonably well for up to 2 weeks in an airtight container.

Nutritional information per portion: Energy 247kcal/1018kJ; Protein 4.1g; Carbohydrate 0g, of which sugars 0g; Fat 25g, of which saturates 6.4g; Cholesterol 28mg; Calcium 3mg; Fibre 0g; Sodium 20mg.

PinchitosMoruños

The Moors introduced both skewers and marinated meat to Spain. These little yellow kebabs are a favourite in Andalusia, where many butchers sell the meat ready marinated. The Arab versions used lamb, but pork is used now, because the spicing fits so perfectly.

SERVES 4

2.5ml/1/2 tsp cumin seeds
2.5ml/1/2 tsp coriander seeds
2 garlic cloves, finely chopped
5ml/1 tsp paprika
2.5ml/1/2 tsp dried oregano
15ml/1 tbsp lemon juice
45ml/3 tbsp olive oil
500g/11/4lb lean cubed pork
salt and ground black pepper

Directions

1 Starting a couple of hours in advance, grind the cumin and coriander seeds in a mortar and work in the garlic with a pinch of salt. Add the paprika and oregano and mix in the lemon juice. Stir in the oil.

2 Cut the pork into small cubes, then skewer them, three or four at a time, on to cocktail sticks (toothpicks). Put the skewered meat in a shallow dish,

and pour over the marinade. Spoon the marinade back over the meat to ensure that it is well coated. Leave to marinate in a cool place for 2 hours.

3 Preheat the grill (broiler) to high, and line the grill pan with foil. Spread the kebabs out in a row and place under the grill, close to the heat. Cook for about 3 minutes on each side, spooning the juices over when you turn them, until cooked through. Sprinkle with salt and pepper, and serve.

Nutritional information per portion: Energy 233kcal/970kJ; Protein 27g; Carbohydrate 0.7g, of which sugars 0g; Fat 13.5g, of which saturates 2.9g; Cholesterol 79mg; Calcium 25mg; Fibre 0.6g; Sodium 99mg.

Soups and Eggs

Gazpacho is a world-famous soup, but there are many other delicious recipes, from light dishes to hearty soups that are meals in themselves. Tortilla is the quintessential Spanish dish, and eggs hold a special place in the Spanish heart – for they symbolize the countryside, where many dream of setting up home.

Gazpacho

This classic chilled soup is deeply rooted in Andalusia. The flavoursome blend of tomatoes, sweet peppers and garlic is sharpened with sherry vinegar, and enriched with olive oil. Serving it with saucerfuls of garnishes has virtually become a tradition.

SERVES 4

1.3–1.6kg/3–31/2lb ripe tomatoes
1 green (bell) pepper, seeded and roughly chopped
2 garlic cloves, finely chopped
2 slices stale bread, crusts removed
60ml/4 tbsp extra virgin olive oil
60ml/4 tbsp sherry vinegar
150ml/1/4 pint/2/3 cup tomato juice
300ml/1/2 pint/11/4 cups iced water

salt and ground black pepper
ice cubes, to serve (optional)

FOR THE GARNISHES
30ml/2 tbsp olive oil
2–3 slices stale bread, diced
1 small cucumber, peeled and finely diced
1 small onion, finely chopped
1 red and 1 green (bell) pepper, seeded and finely diced
2 hard-boiled eggs, chopped

Directions

1 Skin the tomatoes, then quarter them and remove the cores and seeds, saving the juices. Put the pepper in a food processor and process for a few seconds. Add the tomatoes, reserved juices, garlic, bread, oil and vinegar and process. Add the tomato juice and blend until it is combined.

2 Season the soup, then pour into a large bowl, cover with clear film (plastic wrap) and chill for at least 12 hours.

3 Prepare the garnishes. Heat the olive oil in a frying pan and fry the bread cubes for 4–5 minutes until golden brown and crisp. Drain well on kitchen paper, then arrange in a small dish. Place the remaining garnishes in separate small dishes.

4 Just before serving, dilute the soup with the ice-cold water. The consistency should be thick but not stodgy.

If you like, stir a few ice cubes into the soup, then serve with the garnishes.

Nutritional information per portion: Energy 376kcal/1584kJ; Protein 11.3g; Carbohydrate 38.3g, of which sugars 31.3g; Fat 21.1g, of which saturates 3.6g; Cholesterol 95mg; Calcium 109mg; Fibre 8.3g; Sodium 103mg.

Chilled Almond Soup with Grapes

Called ajoblanco – white garlic soup – in Spain, this is a chilled Moorish soup of ancient origin. It is a perfect balance of three southern ingredients: crushed almonds, garlic and vinegar, in a smooth purée made luscious with oil.

SERVES 6

115g/4oz stale white bread
115g/4oz/1 cup blanched almonds
2 garlic cloves, sliced
75ml/5 tbsp olive oil
25ml/11/2 tbsp sherry vinegar
salt and ground black pepper

FOR THE GARNISH
toasted flaked (sliced) almonds
green and black grapes, halved and seeded
chopped fresh chives

Directions

1 Break the bread into a bowl and pour in 150ml/1/4 pint/2/3 cup cold water. Leave to soak for about 5 minutes, then squeeze dry.

2 Put the almonds and garlic in a food processor or blender and process until very finely ground. Add the

soaked white bread and process again until thoroughly combined.

3 Continue to process, gradually adding the oil until the mixture forms a smooth paste. Add the sherry vinegar, followed by 600ml/1 pint/21/2 cups cold water and process until the mixture is smooth.

4 Transfer the soup to a bowl and season with plenty of salt and pepper, adding a little more water if the soup is very thick. Cover with clear film (plastic wrap) and chill for at least 2 hours.

5 Ladle the soup into bowls. Sprinkle the almonds, halved grapes and chopped chives over to garnish.

Nutritional information per portion: Energy 246kcal/1023kJ; Protein 5.8g; Carbohydrate 11.1g, of which sugars 1.3g; Fat 20.2g, of which saturates 2.2g; Cholesterol 0mg; Calcium 67mg; Fibre 1.8g; Sodium103mg.

Catalan Broad Bean and Potato Soup

Habas are fresh broad beans, and are much nicer than the dried variety,known as favas. The word has vanished from the Spanish dictionary and the dried bean has all but disappeared as well. This soup also uses an uncommon herb in Spanish cooking – coriander – but it adds a delicious flavour.

SERVES 4

30ml/2 tbsp olive oil
2 onions, chopped
3 large floury potatoes, peeled and diced
450g/1lb fresh shelled broad (US fava) beans, plus extra to garnish
1.75 litres/3 pints/71/2 cups vegetable stock
1 bunch fresh coriander (cilantro), roughly chopped
150ml/1/4 pint/2/3 cup single (light) cream, plus a little extra to garnish
salt and ground black pepper

Directions

1 Heat the oil in a large pan and fry the onions, stirring, for 5 minutes until soft. Add the potatoes, most of the beans (reserving a few for the garnish) and the stock, and bring to the boil. Simmer for 5 minutes, then add the coriander and simmer for a further 10 minutes.

2 Blend the soup in batches in a food processor or blender, then return to the rinsed pan.
3 Stir in the cream, season to taste, and bring to a simmer. Serve garnished with beans, cream and coriander sprigs.

Nutritional information per portion: Energy 358kcal/1504kJ; Protein 14.3g; Carbohydrate 46.4g, of which sugars 10.1g; Fat 14.2g, of which saturates 5.6g; Cholesterol 21mg; Calcium 156mg; Fibre 10.9g; Sodium 44mg.

Chilled Avocado Soup with Cumin

Andalusia is home to both avocados and gazpacho, so it is not surprising that this chilled avocado soup, which is also known as green gazpacho, was invented there. In Spain, this deliciously mild, creamy soup is known as sopa de aguacate.

SERVES 4

3 ripe avocados
1 bunch spring onions (scallions), white parts only, trimmed and
roughly chopped
2 garlic cloves, chopped
juice of 1 lemon
1.5ml/1/4 tsp ground cumin
1.5ml/1/4 tsp paprika
450ml/3/4 pint/scant 2 cups fresh chicken stock, cooled, and all fat
skimmed off
300ml/1/2 pint/11/4 cups iced water
salt and ground black pepper
chopped fresh flat leaf parsley, to serve

Directions

1 Starting half a day ahead, put the flesh of one avocado in a food processor or blender. Add the spring onions, garlic and lemon juice and purée until smooth. Add the

second avocado and purée, then the third, with the spices and seasoning. Purée until smooth.
2 Gradually add the stock. Pour the soup into a bowl and chill it for several hours.
3 To serve, stir in the iced water, then season to taste with plenty of salt and black pepper. Garnish with chopped parsley and then serve.

Nutritional information per portion: Energy 151kcal/623kJ; Protein 2.1g; Carbohydrate 2.6g, of which sugars 1.1g; Fat 14.6g, of which saturates 3.1g; Cholesterol 0mg; Calcium 19mg; Fibre 3g; Sodium 6mg.

Sopa De Mariscos

This Mediterranean seafood soup can be served as a main course for four or it can be diluted with white wine and water to make an appetizer for six.

SERVES 4

675g/11/2lb raw prawns (shrimp), in the shell
900ml/11/2 pints/33/4 cups cold water
1 onion, chopped
1 celery stick, chopped
1 bay leaf
45ml/3 tbsp olive oil
2 slices stale bread, crusts removed
1 small onion, finely chopped
1 large garlic clove, chopped
2 large tomatoes, halved
1/2 large green (bell) pepper, finely chopped
500g/11/4lb cockles (small clams) or mussels, cleaned
juice of 1 lemon
45ml/3 tbsp chopped fresh parsley
5ml/1 tsp paprika
salt and ground black pepper

Directions

1 Pull the heads off the prawns and put them in a pan with the cold water. Add the onion, celery and bay leaf

and simmer for 20–25 minutes. Peel the prawns, adding the shells to the stock.

2 Heat the oil in a large pan and fry the bread slices quickly, then reserve them. Fry the onion until it is soft, adding the garlic towards the end.

3 Scoop the seeds out of the tomatoes and discard. Chop the flesh and add to the pan with the green pepper. Fry briefly, stirring occasionally. Strain the stock into the pan and bring to the boil. Check over the cockles or mussels, discarding any that are open or damaged.

4 Add half the cockles or mussels to the stock. When open, transfer some of them out on to a plate. Remove the mussels or cockles from the shells and discard the shells. (You should end up having discarded about half of the shells.)

Meanwhile, repeat the process to cook the remaining cockles or mussels.

5 Return the cockles or mussels to the soup and add the prawns. Add the bread, torn into little pieces, and the lemon juice and chopped parsley. Season to taste with paprika, salt and pepper and stir gently to mix in the bread. Serve.

Nutritional information per portion: Energy 301kcal/1266kJ; Protein 39.5g; Carbohydrate 13.5g, of which sugars 6.3g; Fat 10.3g, of which saturates 1.6g; Cholesterol 362mg; Calcium 223mg; Fibre 1.9g; Sodium 709mg.

Sherried Onion Soup with Saffron

The Spanish combination of onions, sherry and saffron gives this pale yellow soup a beguiling taste that is perfect for the opening course of a meal. The addition of ground almonds to thicken the soup gives it a wonderful texture and flavour.

SERVES 4

40g/11/2oz/3 tbsp butter
2 large yellow onions, thinly sliced
1 small garlic clove, finely chopped
pinch of saffron threads (0.25g)
50g/2oz blanched almonds, toasted and finely ground
750ml/11/4 pints/3 cups chicken or vegetable stock
45ml/3 tbsp fino sherry
2.5ml/1/2 tsp paprika
salt and ground black pepper

FOR THE GARNISH
30ml/2 tbsp flaked or sliced almonds, toasted
chopped fresh parsley

Directions

1 Melt the butter in a heavy pan over a low heat. Add the onions and garlic, stirring to ensure that they are

thoroughly coated in the melted butter, then cover the pan and cook very gently, stirring frequently, for about 20 minutes, or until the onions are soft and golden yellow.

2 Add the saffron threads to the pan and cook, uncovered, for 3–4 minutes, then add the finely ground almonds and cook, stirring the ingredients constantly, for a further 2–3 minutes. Pour the chicken or vegetable stock and sherry into the pan and stir in 5ml/1 tsp salt and the paprika. Season with plenty of black pepper.Bring to the boil, then lower the heat and simmer gently for about 10 minutes.

3 Pour the soup into a food processor and process until smooth, then return it to the rinsed pan. Reheat slowly, without allowing the soup to boil, stirring occasionally. Taste for seasoning, adding more salt and pepper if required. Ladle the soup into heated bowls, garnish with the toasted flaked or sliced almonds and a little chopped fresh parsley and serve immediately.

Nutritional information per portion: Energy 246kcal/1017kJ; Protein 5.5g; Carbohydrate 9.5g, of which sugars 6.7g; Fat 19.6g, of which saturates 6.1g; Cholesterol 21mg; Calcium 76mg; Fibre 2.9g; Sodium 68mg.

SopaCastiliana

This rich, dark garlic soup, which comes from La Mancha, a poor region in central Spain, has harsh, strong tastes to match the hot, dry climate. People either love it or hate it. Poaching a whole egg in each bowl just before serving transforms the soup into a meal.

SERVES 4

30ml/2 tbsp olive oil
4 large garlic cloves, peeled
4 slices stale country bread
20ml/4 tsp paprika
1 litre/13/4 pints/4 cups beef stock
1.5ml/1/4 tsp ground cumin
4 eggs
salt and ground black pepper
chopped fresh parsley, to garnish

Directions

1 Preheat the oven to 230°C/450°F/Gas 8. Heat the olive oil in a large pan. Add the whole peeled garlic cloves and cook gently until they are golden, then remove and set aside. Fry the slices of bread in the oil until they are golden, then set these aside.

2 Add 15ml/1 tbsp of the paprika to the pan, and fry for a few seconds. Stir in the beef stock, cumin and remaining paprika, then add the reserved garlic, crushing the cloves with the back of a wooden spoon. Season to taste, then cook for about 5 minutes.
3 Break up the slices of fried bread into bitesize pieces and stir them into the soup. Ladle the soup into four ovenproof bowls. Carefully break an egg into each bowl of soup and place in the oven for about 3 minutes, until the eggs are set. Sprinkle the soup with chopped fresh parsley and serve immediately.

Nutritional information per portion: Energy 208kcal/870kJ; Protein 9.5g; Carbohydrate 16.5g, of which sugars 0.8g; Fat 12.3g, of which saturates 2.4g; Cholesterol 190mg; Calcium 71mg; Fibre 0.5g; Sodium 228mg.

Fish Soup with Orange

The old name for this soup is sopacachorreña – Seville orange soup – and it is good served post-Christmas, when Seville oranges are in season. It has a beautiful orange colour. The fish used is normally small hake, but any white fish is suitable.

SERVES 6

1kg/21/4lb small hake or whiting, whole but cleaned
1.2 litres/2 pints/5 cups water
4 bitter oranges or 4 sweet oranges and 2 lemons
30ml/2 tbsp olive oil
5 garlic cloves, unpeeled
1 large onion, finely chopped
1 tomato, peeled, seeded and chopped
4 small potatoes, cut into rounds
5ml/1 tsp paprika
salt and ground black pepper
15–30ml/1–2 tbsp finely chopped fresh parsley, to garnish

Directions

1 Fillet the fish and cut each fillet into three, reserving all the trimmings. Put the fillets on a plate, salt lightly and chill. Put the trimmings in a pan, add the water and a spiral of orange rind. Bring to a simmer, skim, then cover and cook gently for 30 minutes.

2 Heat the oil in a large pan over a high heat. Smash the garlic cloves with the flat of a knife and fry until they are well coloured. Discard them and turn down the heat. Fry the onion gently until it is softened, adding the tomato halfway through.

3 Strain in the hot fish stock (adding the orange spiral as well if you wish) and bring back to the boil. Add the potatoes to the pan and cook them for about 5minutes.

4 Add the fish pieces to the soup, a few at a time, without letting it go off the boil. Cook for about 15 minutes. Add the squeezed orange juice and lemon juice, if using, and the paprika, with salt and pepper to taste. Serve in bowls, garnished with a little parsley.

Nutritional information per portion: Energy 223kcal/937kJ; Protein 18.3g; Carbohydrate 25.2g, of which sugars 11.7g; Fat 6.1g, of which saturates 0.9g; Cholesterol 19mg; Calcium 86mg; Fibre 3.5g; Sodium 103mg.

Spicy Sausage and Cheese Tortilla

This substantial tortilla is delicious hot or cold. Cut it into wedges and serve for supper with a tomato and basil salad. Adding spicy chorizo and tangy cheese gives it a wonderful, rich flavour.

SERVES 4–6

75ml/5 tbsp olive oil
175g/6oz frying chorizo or spicy sausage, thinly sliced
675g/11/2lb waxy potatoes, thinly sliced
2 Spanish onions, halved and thinly sliced
4 large (US extra large) eggs
30ml/2 tbsp chopped fresh parsley, plus extra to garnish
115g/4oz/1 cup grated Cheddar or other hard cheese
salt and ground black pepper

Directions

1 Heat 15ml/1 tbsp of the oil in a 23cm/9in frying pan and fry the sausage until golden and cooked through. Drain on kitchen paper.

2 Add a further 30ml/2 tbsp oil to the pan and fry the potatoes and onions for 2–3 minutes, turning frequently. Cover tightly and cook over a gentle heat for about 30 minutes, turning occasionally, until softened and slightly golden.

3 In a large mixing bowl, beat together the eggs, parsley, cheese, sausage and plenty of seasoning. Gently stir in the potatoes and onions until coated.
4 Wipe out the pan with kitchen paper and heat the remaining 30ml/2 tbsp oil. Add the potato mixture and cook, over a very low heat, until the egg begins to set. Use a metal spatula to prevent the tortilla sticking and to allow the uncooked egg to run underneath.
5 Preheat the grill (broiler) to high. When the base of the tortilla has set, which should take about 5 minutes, protect the pan handle with foil and place thetortilla under the grill until it is set and golden. Cut into wedges and servegarnished with parsley.

Nutritional information per portion: Energy 409kcal/1703kJ; Protein 14.9g; Carbohydrate 28.3g, of which sugars 6.8g; Fat 26.7g, of which saturates 9.5g; Cholesterol 157mg; Calcium 212mg; Fibre 2.7g; Sodium 438mg.

Tortilla with Beans

The addition of chopped herbs and skinned beans to the classic tortilla makes this a very summery dish. Enjoy it for lunch, or cut it into small pieces and serve as tapas.

SERVES 2

45ml/3 tbsp olive oil
2 Spanish onions, thinly sliced
300g/11oz waxy potatoes, cut into dice
250g/9oz/13/4 cups shelled broad (fava) beans
5ml/1 tsp chopped fresh thyme or summer savory
6 large (US extra large) eggs
45ml/3 tbsp mixed chopped fresh chives and fresh flat leaf parsley
salt and ground black pepper

Directions

1 Heat 30ml/2 tbsp of the oil in a 23cm/9in deep non-stick frying pan. Add the onions and potatoes and stir to coat. Cover and cook gently, stirring, for 20–25 minutes until the potatoes are cooked.
2 Meanwhile, cook the beans in a pan of boiling salted water for 5 minutes. Drain and set aside to cool.
3 When the beans are cool enough to handle, peel off and discard the grey outer skins. Add the beans to the frying pan, together with the thyme or summer savory,

and season to taste. Stir well to mix and cook for a further 2–3 minutes.

4 Beat the eggs with salt and pepper to taste and add the mixed herbs, then pourover the potatoes and onions and increase the heat. Cook gently for 5 minutes, or until the bottom browns. During cooking, pull the tortilla away from the sides of the pan and tilt it to allow the uncooked egg to run underneath.

5 Cover the pan with a plate and invert the tortilla on to it. Add the remaining oilto the pan and heat. Slip the tortilla back into the pan, uncooked side down, and cook for 3–5 minutes until the underneath turns brown. Slide the tortilla out on to a plate. Cut it up and serve warm.

Nutritional information per portion: Energy 637kcal/2662kJ; Protein 33.7g; Carbohydrate 51.3g, of which sugars 12.5g; Fat 35g, of which saturates 7.3g; Cholesterol 571mg; Calcium 247mg; Fibre 12.9g; Sodium 249mg.

Potato Tortilla

The classic tortilla stands on every tapas bar in Spa. The size of a large cake, it is very satisfying. It can be eaten in wedges – a meal in itself with salad – or cut into chunks and enjoyed as a snack.

SERVES 6

450g/1lb small waxy potatoes, peeled
1 Spanish onion
45ml/3 tbsp vegetable oil
4 large (US extra large) eggs
salt and ground black pepper
fresh flat leaf parsley or tomato wedges, to garnish

Directions

1 Using a sharp knife, cut the potatoes into thin slices and slice the onion into thin rings. Heat 30ml/2 tbsp of the oil in a 20cm/8in heavy frying pan.

2 Add the potatoes and the onions to the pan and cook over a low heat for 20 minutes, or until the potato slices are just tender. Remove from the heat.

3 In a large bowl, beat together the eggs with a little salt and pepper. Stir in the potatoes and onion.

4 Clean the frying pan with kitchen paper then heat the remaining oil and pour in the potato mixture. Cook very gently for 5–8 minutes until set underneath. During cooking, lift the edges of the tortilla with a spatula, and allow any uncooked egg to run

underneath. Shake the pan from side to side, to prevent sticking.

5 Place a large heatproof plate upside-down over the pan, invert the tortilla on to the plate and then slide it back into the pan. Cook for 2–3 minutes more, until the underside of the tortilla is golden brown. Cut into wedges and serve, garnished with fresh flat leaf parsley or tomato wedges.

Nutritional information per portion: Energy 163kcal/681kJ; Protein 5.8g; Carbohydrate 14.7g, of which sugars 2.8g; Fat 9.5g, of which saturates 1.9g; Cholesterol 127mg; Calcium 32mg; Fibre 1.2g; Sodium 56mg.

Flamenco Eggs

This dish is a swirl of red, green, yellow and white – as colourful as the skirts of flamenco dancers. It uses whatever ingredients are available, for example, peas in spring or squash later in the year.

SERVES 4

30ml/2 tbsp olive oil
115g/4oz smoked bacon lardons or diced pancetta
2 frying chorizos, cubed
1 onion, chopped
2 garlic cloves, finely chopped
1 red and 1 green (bell) pepper, seeded and chopped
500g/11/4lb tomatoes, chopped
15–30ml/1–2 tbsp fino sherry
45ml/3 tbsp chopped fresh parsley
8 large (US extra large) eggs
salt, paprika and cayenne

FOR THE MIGAS
4 thick slices stale bread
oil, for frying
2 garlic cloves, bruised

Directions

1 Preheat the oven to 180°C/350°F/Gas 4. Warm four individual baking dishes.

2 Heat the oil in a frying pan and fry the bacon or pancetta and chorizos, to give off their fat. Add the onion and garlic and cook gently until softened, stirring. Add the peppers and tomatoes and cook until reduced, stirring occasionally. Add some paprika and sherry.

3 Divide the mixture evenly among the baking dishes. Sprinkle with parsley.Swirl the eggs together with a fork and season well with salt and cayenne. Pourover the mixture. Bake the eggs and vegetables for 8 minutes, or until the eggs are just set.

4 Meanwhile make the migas. Cut the crusts off the bread and reduce to crumbs in a food processor.

5 Heat plenty of oil in a frying pan over a high heat, add the garlic cloves for a few moments to flavour it, then discard them. Throw in the crumbs and brown quickly, scooping them out on to kitchen paper. Season with a little salt and paprika, then sprinkle around the edge of the eggs to serve.

Nutritional information per portion: Energy 592kcal/2464kJ; Protein 26.6g; Carbohydrate 30.4g, of which sugars 12g; Fat 41.1g, of which saturates 11.8g; Cholesterol 416mg; Calcium 155mg; Fibre 4.1g; Sodium 1150mg

Scrambled Eggs with Prawns

The Spanish distinguish between a revuelto, which uses softly-set scrambled eggs, and the more solid tortilla that is cooked until set. This revuelto de gambas is a good way of using shellfish.

SERVES 4

1 bunch spring onions (scallions)
25g/1oz/2 tbsp butter
30ml/2 tbsp oil
150g/5oz shelled prawns (shrimp)
8 large (US extra large) eggs
30ml/2 tbsp milk
45ml/3 tbsp chopped fresh parsley
salt and ground black pepper
crusty bread, to serve

Directions

1 Chop the white of the spring onions and reserve, keeping it separate from 30ml/2 tbsp of the green tops.
2 Heat the butter and oil in a large frying pan. Add the spring onion white and cook briefly. Add the prawns and heat through. (If the prawns are raw, then cook them for 2 minutes.)
3 Beat the eggs with the milk and then season. Turn the heat to medium-high and pour the egg mixture over the prawns. Cook for about 2 minutes, stirring with a wooden spoon.

4 Sprinkle with parsley and spring onion greens. Divide among four plates and serve immediately with crusty bread.

Nutritional information per portion: Energy 285kcal/1182kJ; Protein 20.2g; Carbohydrate 1.5g, of which sugars 1.4g; Fat 22.4g, of which saturates 7.3g; Cholesterol 467mg; Calcium 129mg; Fibre 1g; Sodium 258mg.

Scrambled Eggs with Spring Asparagus

Revuelto de espárragos is one of those delicious egg dishes that show off new green spring vegetables to perfection. Tender fresh asparagus and mangetouts are perfect partners to the eggs.

SERVES 4

1 bunch thin asparagus
30–45ml/2–3 tbsp mangetouts (snow peas)
8 large (US extra large) eggs
30ml/2 tbsp milk
50g/2oz/1/4 cup butter
salt and ground black pepper
sweet paprika, for dusting

Directions

1 Prepare the asparagus. Using a sharp knife, cut off and discard any hard stems. Cut the stems, keeping the tips separate. Shell some of the fatter mangetout pods, to extract the peas, and cut the pods into strips, if you like.

2 Put the stems into a pan of boiling water and simmer for 4 minutes. Add the asparagus tips, and cook for another 6 minutes. If including some pea pod strips, cook them for 2 minutes. Break the eggs into a bowl and beat together with the milk, salt and black pepper.

3 Melt the butter in a frying pan and pour in the eggs, scrambling them by pulling the cooked outsides to the middle with a wooden spoon. When the eggs are almost cooked, drain the asparagus and pea pod strips, if using, and stir into the eggs. Sprinkle the peas over the top, dust with paprika and serve.

Nutritional information per portion: Energy 262kcal/1085kJ; Protein 14.9g; Carbohydrate 2.2g, of whichsugars 1.4g; Fat 21.9g, of which saturates 9.7g; Cholesterol 407mg; Calcium 78mg; Fibre 1.4g; Sodium 217mg.

Pan-Fried Ham and Vegetables with Eggs

Little vegetable dishes, and ones that contain ham or eggs, or both, are the backbone of the Spanish supper scene. This delicious dish is easy to make and it is hearty enough to serve as a meal in itself with a simple salad.

SERVES 4

30ml/2 tbsp olive oil
1 onion, roughly chopped
2 garlic cloves, finely chopped
175g/6oz cooked ham
225g/8oz courgettes (zucchini)
1 red (bell) pepper, seeded and thinly sliced
1 yellow (bell) pepper, seeded and thinly sliced
10ml/2 tsp paprika
400g/14oz can chopped tomatoes
15ml/1 tbsp sun-dried tomato paste
4 large (US extra large) eggs
115g/4oz/1 cup coarsely grated Cheddar cheese
salt and ground black pepper
crusty bread, to serve

Directions

1 Heat the olive oil in a deep frying pan. Add the onion and garlic and cook for 4 minutes, stirring frequently.

2 Meanwhile, cut the cooked ham and courgettes into 5cm/2in batons.
3 Add the courgettes and peppers to the pan and cook over a medium heat for 3–4 minutes.
4 Stir in the paprika, tomatoes, tomato paste, ham and seasoning. Bring to a simmer and cook over a gentle heat for 15 minutes.
5 Reduce the heat to low. Make four wells in the tomato mixture, break an egginto each and season. Cook over a gentle heat until the white begins to set. Preheat the grill (broiler). Sprinkle the cheese over and grill (broil) for about 5 minutes until the eggs are set. Serve with crusty bread.

Nutritional information per portion: Energy 357kcal/1487kJ; Protein 24.8g; Carbohydrate 12.2g, of which sugars 10.7g; Fat 23.1g, of which saturates 9.4g; Cholesterol 244mg; Calcium 280mg; Fibre 3.1g; Sodium 817mg.

Vegetables

Salads start the meal in summer, and typify Spain's attitude to cooking, using fresh, local seasonal ingredients. Vegetable dishes are inventive too, eaten as tapas, a course on their own, or perhaps as a supper. Vegetables and salads are often embellished with chorizo, bacon lardons, tuna or hard-boiled eggs to add flavour and make a more substantial dish.

Ensaladilla

Ensaladilla known as Russian salad elsewhere, this "salad of little things" became extremely popular during the Spanish Civil War in the 1930s, when more expensive ingredients were scarce.

SERVES 4

8 new potatoes, scrubbed and quartered
1 large carrot, diced
115g/4oz fine green beans, cut into 2cm/3/4in lengths
75g/3oz/3/4 cup peas
1/2 Spanish onion, chopped
4 cornichons or small gherkins, sliced
1 small red (bell) pepper, seeded and diced
50g/2oz/1/2 cup pitted black olives

15ml/1 tbsp drained pickled capers
15ml/1 tbsp freshly squeezed lemon juice
30ml/2 tbsp chopped fennel or parsley
salt and ground black pepper

FOR THE AIOLI
2 garlic cloves, finely chopped
2.5ml/1/2 tsp salt
150ml/1/4 pint/2/3 cup mayonnaise

Directions

1 To make the aioli, crush the garlic with the salt in a mortar and whisk or stir into the mayonnaise.
2 Cook the potatoes and diced carrot in a pan of boiling lightly salted water for 5–8 minutes until almost tender. Add the beans and peas to the pan and cook for 2 minutes, or until all the vegetables are tender. Drain well.
3 Put the vegetables into a large bowl. Add the onion, cornichons or gherkins, red pepper, olives and capers. Stir in the aioli and season to taste with the black pepper and the lemon juice.
4 Toss the vegetables and aioli together until well combined, check the seasoning and chill well. Serve garnished with fennel or parsley.

Nutritional information per portion: Energy 494kcal/2045kJ; Protein 5.1g; Carbohydrate 25.6g, of which sugars 8.1g; Fat 42g, of which saturates 6.3g; Cholesterol 28mg; Calcium 60mg; Fibre 4.5g; Sodium

191mg.

Charred Artichokes with Lemon Oil Dip

Young artichokes, alcachofas, are cooked over the first barbecues of the summer. However, they are also very good roasted in the oven.

SERVES 2–4

15ml/1 tbsp lemon juice or white wine vinegar
2 globe artichokes
45ml/3 tbsp olive oil
sea salt
sprigs of fresh flat leaf parsley, to garnish

FOR THE LEMON OIL DIP
12 garlic cloves, unpeeled
1 lemon
45ml/3 tbsp extra virgin olive oil

Directions

1 Preheat the oven to 200°C/400°F/Gas 6. Stir the lemon juice or the vinegar into a bowl of cold water.
2 Cut each artichoke lengthways into wedges. Pull the hairy choke out from the centre of each wedge and drop the wedges into the acidulated water.

3 Drain the artichokes and place in a roasting pan with the garlic cloves. Toss in the oil. Sprinkle with salt and roast for 40 minutes, stirring once or twice, until the artichokes are tender.

4 Meanwhile, make the dip. Pare away two strips of rind from the lemon and scrape away any pith. Place the rind in a pan with water to cover. Simmer for 5 minutes, then drain, refresh in cold water and chop roughly.

5 Arrange the artichokes on a plate and set aside to cool for 5 minutes. Flatten the garlic cloves so that the flesh pops out of the skins. Transfer the garlic flesh to a bowl, mash to a purée then add the lemon rind. Squeeze the juice from the lemon, then, using a fork, whisk in the olive oil and lemon juice.

6 Serve the artichokes warm, garnished with the parsley and accompanied with the dip.

Nutritional information per portion: Energy 166kcal/684kJ; Protein 1.4g; Carbohydrate 2.7g, of which sugars 0.9g; Fat 16.7g, of which saturates 2.4g; Cholesterol 0mg; Calcium 33mg; Fibre 1.3g; Sodium 46mg.

Mushroom, Bean and Chorizo Salad

This really simple salad can be served as an accompaniment to plain fish or chicken dishes, or with crusty bread as a hearty lunch or supper dish. The combination of spicy sausage, beans and mushrooms is delicious.

SERVES 4

225g/8oz shelled broad (fava) beans
175g/6oz frying chorizo
60ml/4 tbsp extra virgin olive oil
225g/8oz/3 cups brown cap (cremini) mushrooms, sliced
60ml/4 tbsp chopped fresh chives
salt and ground black pepper

1 Cook the broad beans in a pan of salted boiling water for 7–8 minutes. Drain and refresh under cold water.
2 Remove the skin from the sausage. If it doesn't peel off easily, score along the length of the sausage with a sharp knife first. Cut the chorizo into small chunks. Heat thc oil in a small pan, add the chorizo and cook for 2–3 minutes.
3 Put the sliced mushrooms in a bowl and add the chorizo and oil. Toss to combine then leave to cool.

4 If the beans are large, peel away the tough outer skins. Stir the beans and half the chives into the mushroom mixture, and season to taste. Serve at room temperature, garnished with the remaining chives.

Nutritional information per portion: Energy 166kcal/684kJ; Protein 1.4g; Carbohydrate 2.7g, of which sugars 0.9g; Fat 16.7g, of which saturates 2.4g; Cholesterol 0mg; Calcium 33mg; Fibre 1.3g; Sodium 46mg.

Avocado, Orange and Almond Salad

In Andalusia, avocados have become one of the big cash crops, replacing many orange orchards. In this salad, ensalada de aguacates, the smooth, creamy avocados combine perfectly with local oranges and almonds.

SERVES 4

2–3 oranges
2 ripe tomatoes
2 small avocados
60ml/4 tbsp extra virgin olive oil
30ml/2 tbsp lemon juice
15ml/1 tbsp chopped fresh parsley
1 small onion, cut into rings
25g/1oz/1/4 cup split, toasted almonds
10–12 black olives
salt and ground black pepper

Directions

1 Peel the oranges and slice them into thick rounds. Plunge the tomatoes into boiling water for 30 seconds, then refresh in cold water. Peel away the skins, cut the tomatoes into quarters, remove the seeds and chop them roughly. Cut the avocados in half, remove the

stones (pits) and carefully peel away the skin. Cut into chunks.

2 Mix together the olive oil, lemon juice and parsley. Season with salt and
pepper, then toss the avocados and tomatoes in half of the dressing.

3 Arrange the oranges on a plate and add the onion rings. Drizzle with the remaining dressing. Spoon over avocados, tomatoes, almonds and olives and serve.

Nutritional information per portion: Energy 295kcal/1224kJ; Protein 4g; Carbohydrate 12.5g, of which sugars 11.6g; Fat 25.8g, of which saturates 4.2g; Cholesterol 0mg; Calcium 85mg; Fibre 5g; Sodium 295mg.

La Calçotada

Spring onions – calçot in Spanish – have their own festival in the province of Tarragona. It is a day to mark the return of better weather, and in the past, the onions were barbecued in the fields.

SERVES 6

3 bunches of plump spring onions (scallions), or Chinese green onions,
which are about 2.5cm/1in across the bulb
olive oil, for brushing

FOR THE ROMESCO SAUCE
2–3 ñoras or other mild dried red chillies, such as Mexican anchos orguajillos
1 large red (bell) pepper, halved and seeded
2 large tomatoes, halved and seeded
4–6 large garlic cloves, unpeeled
75–90ml/5–6 tbsp olive oil
25g/1oz/1/4 cup hazelnuts, blanched
4 slices French bread, each about 2cm/3/4in thick
15ml/1 tbsp sherry vinegar
squeeze of lemon juice (optional)

Directions

1 Soak the dried chillies in hot water for about 30 minutes. Preheat the oven to 220°C/425°F/Gas 7.

Place the pepper, tomatoes and garlic on a baking sheet and drizzle with 15ml/1 tbsp olive oil. Roast, uncovered, for 30–40 minutes, until the pepper is blistered and blackened and the garlic is soft. Cool slightly, then peel the pepper, tomatoes and garlic.

2 Heat the remaining oil in a small frying pan and fry the hazelnuts until lightly browned, then transfer them to a plate. Fry the bread in the same oil until light brown on both sides, then transfer to the plate with the nuts and leave to cool. Reserve the oil from cooking.

3 Drain the chillies, discard as many of their seeds as you can, then place the chillies in a food processor. Add the red pepper halves, tomatoes, garlic, hazelnuts and bread chunks together with the reserved olive oil. Add the vinegar and process to a paste. Check the seasoning and thin the sauce with a little more oil or lemon juice, if necessary. Set aside.

4 Trim the roots from the spring onions or trim the Chinese onion leaves so that they are about 15–18cm/6–7in long. Brush with oil. Heat an oiled ridged griddle and cook the onions for about 2 minutes on each side, turning once and brushing with oil. Serve at once with the sauce.

Nutritional information per portion: Energy 214kcal/896kJ; Protein 5.2g; Carbohydrate 21g, of which sugars 5.3g; Fat 12.8g, of which saturates 1.7g; Cholesterol 0mg; Calcium 64mg; Fibre 2.8g; Sodium 173mg.

Stewed Aubergine

The Arabs introduced this vegetable-fruit to Andalusia, where it was cooked with the Arab flavourings of cumin and garlic. This is a modern version of berenjenaguisada, with red wine.

SERVES 4

1 large aubergine (eggplant)
60–90ml/4–6 tbsp olive oil
2 shallots, thinly sliced
4 tomatoes, quartered
2 garlic cloves, thinly sliced
60ml/4 tbsp red wine
30ml/2 tbsp chopped fresh parsley, plus extra to garnish
30–45ml/2–3 tbsp extra virgin olive oil (if serving cold)
salt and ground black pepper

Directions

1 Slice thc aubergine into 1cm/1/2in rounds. Place them in a large colander and sprinkle with 5–10ml/1–2 tsp salt. Leave to drain for 30 minutes.
2 Rinse the aubergine slices well, then press between several layers of kitchen paper to remove any excess liquid.

3 Heat 30ml/2 tbsp of the oil in a large frying pan until smoking. Add a single layer of aubergine slices and fry, turning once, until golden brown. Remove to a plate covered with kitchen paper to drain. Heat more oil and fry the second batch in the same way.

4 Heat 15ml/1 tbsp of oil in a pan and cook the shallots for 5 minutes until golden. Cut the aubergine into strips. Add, with the tomatoes, garlic and wine. Cover and simmer for 30 minutes.

5 Stir in the parsley, and check the seasonings. Sprinkle with a little more parsleyand serve hot. To serve cold, dribble a little extra virgin olive oil over the dishbefore it goes on the table.

Nutritional information per portion: Energy 197kcal/816kJ; Protein 2g; Carbohydrate 7.3g, of which sugars 6.7g; Fat 17.3g, of which saturates 2.6g; Cholesterol 0mg; Calcium 23mg; Fibre 3.5g; Sodium 15mg.

Braised Cabbage with Chorizo

Cabbages – berzas – mark the landscape in Galicia, where the huge vegetables grow more than hip high. They are popularly cooked in stews in the many mountain regions of the south, and are frequently served with chickpeas or sausages, as in this recipe.

SERVES 4

50g/2oz/1/4 cup butter
5ml/1 tsp coriander seeds
225g/8oz green cabbage, shredded
2 garlic cloves, finely chopped
50g/2oz cured chorizo sausage, roughly chopped
60ml/4 tbsp dry sherry or white wine
salt and ground black pepper

Directions

1 Melt the butter in a large frying pan, add the coriander seeds and cook for 1 minute. Add the shredded cabbage to the pan with the chopped garlic and chorizo. Stir-fry gently for 5 minutes.
2 Add the sherry or wine and plenty of salt and pepper to the pan. Cover and cook for 15–20 minutes until the cabbage is tender. Check the seasoning, adding more if necessary, and then serve.

Nutritional information per portion: Energy 163kcal/673kJ; Protein 2.1g; Carbohydrate 4.6g, of which sugars 3.3g; Fat 13.4g, of which saturates 7.8g; Cholesterol 32mg; Calcium 37mg; Fibre 1.3g; Sodium183mg.

Broad Beans with Bacon

This dish is associated with Ronda, in southern Spain, the home of bullfighting, where broad beans are fed to the bulls to build them up. It is also found elsewhere in Spain where it is known as habasespañolas. If you have time, remove the outer dull skins from the broad beans.

SERVES 4

30ml/2 tbsp olive oil
1 small onion, finely chopped
1 garlic clove, finely chopped
50g/2oz rindless smoked streaky (fatty) bacon, roughly chopped
225g/8oz broad (fava) beans, thawed if frozen
5ml/1 tsp paprika
15ml/1 tbsp sweet sherry
salt and ground black pepper

Directions

1 Heat the olive oil in a large frying pan or sauté pan. Add the chopped onion, garlic and bacon and fry over a high heat for about 5 minutes, stirring frequently, until the onion is softened and the bacon browned.
2 Add the beans and paprika to the pan and stir-fry for 1 minute. Add the sherry, lower the heat, cover and

cook for 5–10 minutes until the beans are tender. Season with salt and pepper and serve hot or warm.

Nutritional information per portion: Energy 139kcal/577kJ; Protein 6.8g; Carbohydrate 8.2g, of which sugars 1.6g; Fat 9g, of which saturates 1.9g; Cholesterol 8mg; Calcium 38mg; Fibre 3.9g; Sodium 163mg.

Amanida

The word amanida is Catalan for an arranged salad that includes fish, meat and vegetables in equal proportions. These salads can be a wonder to behold, but are also simple to make.

SERVES 6

1 lolla green lettuce
50g/2oz cured, sliced chorizo or in a piece skinned and diced
4 thin slices Serrano ham
130g/41/2oz can sardines in oil, drained
130g/41/2oz can tuna steak in oil, drained
8 canned white asparagus spears, drained
2–3 canned palm hearts, drained
115g/4oz/2/3 cup tiny arbequina olives
115g/4oz/2/3 cup big gordas or queen olives, preferably purplish ones
10 medium tomatoes
15ml/1 tbsp chopped fresh parsley, to garnish

FOR THE VINAIGRETTE
1 garlic clove, split lengthways
30ml/2 tbsp sherry vinegar
30ml/2 tbsp red wine vinegar
60ml/4 tbsp olive oil
60ml/4 tbsp extra virgin olive oil

salt and ground black pepper

Directions

1 Make the vinaigrette. Wipe the cut side of the garlic round a large bowl, thendiscard. Whisk the other ingredients together in the bowl.

2 Break the stem ends off eight lettuce leaves, dip the leaves into the vinaigrette and arrange them around a large serving plate.

3 Position the chorizo slices or dice on one side of the plate. Roll the ham andarrange opposite. Drain and blot the fish, then arrange across the plate in a cross. Put the asparagus, spears outwards, and the palm hearts (split lengthways), on opposite sides of the plate. Pile the olives in the spaces.

4 Put the tomatoes in a bowl and pour over boiling water. Leave to stand for 10 minutes, then drain. Peel and quarter six of the tomatoes and cut out the centres. Arrange the tomatoes, round side up, in the centre of the plate to make a flower shape. Brush vinaigrette dressing over the tomatoes, palm hearts and asparagus and season lightly. Sprinkle the parsley on the tomatoes and white vegetables. Serve at room temperature.

Nutritional information per portion: Energy 638kcal/2671kJ; Protein 74.6g; Carbohydrate 9.8g, of which sugars 9.8g; Fat 33.7g, of which saturates 7.3g; Cholesterol 218mg; Calcium 183mg; Fibre 3.1g; Sodium 4618mg.

Patatas Bravas

There are several variations on this chilli and potato dish, but the most
important thing is the spicing, which is made hotter still by adding vinegar. The name bravas implies that the potatoes are so hot that it is manly to eat them.

SERVES 4

675g/11/2lb small new potatoes
75ml/5 tbsp olive oil
2 garlic cloves, sliced
3 dried chillies, seeded and chopped
2.5ml/1/2 tsp ground cumin
10ml/2 tsp paprika
30ml/2 tbsp red or white wine vinegar
1 red or green (bell) pepper, seeded and sliced
coarse sea salt, for sprinkling (optional)

Directions

1 Scrub the potatoes and put them into a pan of salted water. Bring to the boil and cook for 10 minutes, or until almost tender. Drain and leave to cool slightly. Peel, if you like, then cut into chunks.

2 Heat the oil in a frying or sauté pan and fry the potatoes, turning them
frequently, until golden.

3 Meanwhile, crush together the garlic cloves, the chillies and cumin using a mortar and pestle. Mix the

paste with the paprika and wine vinegar, then add to the potatoes with the pepper and cook, stirring, for 2 minutes. Sprinkle with salt, if using, and serve hot as a tapas dish or cold as a side dish.

Nutritional information per portion: Energy 256kcal/1070kJ; Protein 3.3g; Carbohydrate 30g, of which sugars 4.9g; Fat 14.4g, of which saturates 2.2g; Cholesterol 0mg; Calcium 14mg; Fibre 2.4g; Sodium 20mg.

Escalivada

The Catalan name of this celebrated dish means "baked over embers" and, like many other barbecue dishes, it transfers very successfully to the oven. Cooking the vegetables in this way brings out their flavour magnificently.

SERVES 4

2–3 courgettes (zucchini)
1 large fennel bulb
1 Spanish onion
2 large red (bell) peppers
450g/1lb butternut squash
6 whole garlic cloves, unpeeled
75ml/5 tbsp olive oil
juice of 1/2 lemon
pinch of cumin seeds, crushed
4 sprigs fresh thyme
4 medium tomatoes, halved
salt and ground black pepper

Directions

1 Preheat the oven to 220°C/425°F/Gas 7. Cut the courgettes lengthways into four pieces. Cut the fennel into similar-sized wedges. Slice the onion lengthways into chunks. Halve and seed the peppers, and slice thickly lengthways. Cut the squash into thick chunks.

Smash the garlic cloves with the flat of a knife, but leave the skins on.

2 Choose a roasting pan into which all the vegetables will fit in one layer. Put in all the vegetables except the tomatoes. Mix together the olive oil and lemon juice. Pour over the vegetables and toss them. Sprinkle with the cumin seeds, salt and pepper and tuck in the thyme sprigs. Roast for 20 minutes.

3 Gently stir the vegetables in the oil and add the tomatoes. Cook for a further 15 minutes, or until the vegetables are tender and slightly charred around the edges.

Nutritional information per portion: Energy 209kcal/864kJ; Protein 4.6g; Carbohydrate 14.3g, of which sugars 13g; Fat 15.1g, of which saturates 2.4g; Cholesterol 0mg; Calcium 86mg; Fibre 5.6g; Sodium 17mg.

Stuffed Tomatoes and Peppers

Colourful peppers and tomatoes make perfect containers for a simple rice, nut and herb stuffing. The vegetables become deliciously sweet and juicy when baked. Serve tomates y pimientas rellenos as a substantial appetizer or a supper dish.

SERVES 4

2 large tomatoes
1 green (bell) pepper
1 yellow or orange (bell) pepper
75ml/5 tbsp olive oil
2 onions, finely chopped
2 garlic cloves, finely chopped
75g/3oz/3/4 cup almonds, chopped
175g/6oz/11/2 cups cooked rice, or 75g/3oz/scant 1/2 cup long grain rice, cooked and drained
30ml/2 tbsp Malaga raisins or muscatels, soaked in hot water
30ml/2 tbsp chopped fresh mint
45ml/3 tbsp chopped fresh flat leaf parsley, plus extra to garnish
salt and ground black pepper

Directions

1 Preheat the oven to 190°C/375°F/Gas 5. Cut the tomatoes in half and scoop out the pulp and seeds.

2 Put the tomato halves on kitchen paper with the cut sides down and leave to drain. Roughly chop the centres and seeds and place in a bowl.
3 Halve the peppers, leaving the cores intact. Scoop out the seeds. Brush the peppers with 15ml/1 tbsp of the oil.
4 Fry the onions and garlic in 30ml/2 tbsp oil. Stir in most of the almonds. Addthe rice, tomato pulp, drained raisins, mint and 30ml/2 tbsp parsley. Season well,then spoon the mixture into the vegetable cases.
5 Bake uncovered for 20 minutes. Finely chop the remaining almonds and
parsley in a food processor and sprinkle over the top. Drizzle with 15–30ml/1–2 tbsp olive oil. Return to the oven and bake for a further 20 minutes, or until turning golden. Serve, garnished with more chopped parsley.

Nutritional information per portion: Energy 365kcal/1522kJ; Protein 7.1g; Carbohydrate 28.6g, of which sugars 13.7g; Fat 25.5g, of which saturates 3.1g; Cholesterol 0mg; Calcium 95mg; Fibre 3.7g; Sodium
20mg.

Mojete

The Spanish love to scoop up cooked vegetables with bread, and the name of this dish, which is derived from the word meaning to dip, reflects that. Peppers, tomatoes and onions are baked together to make a colourful, soft vegetable dish that is studded with olives.

SERVES 8

2 red (bell) peppers
2 yellow (bell) peppers
1 red onion, sliced
2 garlic cloves, halved
50g/2oz/1/4 cup black olives
6 large ripe tomatoes, quartered
5ml/1 tsp soft light brown sugar
45ml/3 tbsp amontillado sherry
3–4 fresh rosemary sprigs
30ml/2 tbsp olive oil
salt and ground black pepper
fresh bread, to serve

Directions

1 Halve the peppers and remove the seeds. Cut each pepper lengthways into 12 strips. Preheat the oven to 200°C/400°F/Gas 6.

2 Place the peppers, onion, garlic, olives and tomatoes in a large roasting pan.

3 Sprinkle the vegetables with the sugar, thenpour in the sherry. Season well with salt and pepper, cover with foil and bake for 45 minutes.
4 Remove the foil from the pan and stir the mixture well. Add the rosemary sprigs and drizzle with the olive oil. Return the pan to the oven and cook for a further 30 minutes, uncovered, until the vegetables are very tender. Serve hot or cold with chunks of fresh crusty bread.

Nutritional information per portion: Energy 75kcal/313kJ; Protein 1.3g; Carbohydrate 7.5g, of which sugars 7.2g; Fat 3.9g, of which saturates 0.6g; Cholesterol 0mg; Calcium 17mg; Fibre 2g; Sodium 151mg.

Marinated Mushrooms

Champiñonesen escabeche is a good way to serve mushrooms in summer,
and makes a refreshing alternative to the ever-popular mushrooms fried in garlic. Serve with plenty of crusty bread to mop up the delicious juices.

SERVES 4

30ml/2 tbsp olive oil
1 small onion, very finely chopped
1 garlic clove, finely chopped
15ml/1 tbsp tomato purée (paste)
50ml/2fl oz/1/4 cup amontillado sherry
50ml/2fl oz/1/4 cup water
2 cloves
225g/8oz/3 cups button (white) mushrooms, trimmed
salt and ground black pepper
chopped fresh parsley, to garnish

Directions

1 Heat the oil in a pan. Add the onion and garlic and cook until soft. Stir in the tomato purée, sherry, water and cloves, and season to taste. Bring to the boil, cover and simmer gently for 45 minutes. Add more water if it becomes too dry.

2 Add the mushrooms to the pan, then cover and simmer for about 5 minutes. Remove from the heat

and allow to cool, still covered. Chill in the refrigerator overnight. Serve the mushrooms cold, sprinkled with the chopped fresh parsley.

Nutritional information per portion: Energy 80kcal/329kJ; Protein 1.4g; Carbohydrate 2.1g, of which sugars 1.7g; Fat 5.8g, of which saturates 0.9g; Cholesterol 0mg; Calcium 9mg; Fibre 0.9g; Sodium 14mg.

Spinach with Raisins and Pine Nuts

Raisins and pine nuts are frequent partners in Spanish recipes, a combination that was first introduced by the Moors. Here, tossed with wilted spinach and croûtons, they make a delicious snack or main course accompaniment.

SERVES 4

50g/2oz/1/3 cup raisins, preferably Malaga raisins
1 thick slice white bread
45ml/3 tbsp olive oil
25g/1oz/1/4 cup pine nuts
500g/11/4lb young spinach, stalks removed
2 garlic cloves, finely chopped
salt and ground black pepper

Directions

1 Put the raisins in a small bowl and pour over enough boiling water to cover. Leave the raisins to soak for about 10 minutes, then drain well.
2 Cut off the crusts from the white bread and cut into cubes. Heat 30ml/2 tbsp of the oil in a frying pan and fry the cubes of bread until golden. Drain.
3 Heat the remaining oil in the pan. Gently fry the pine nuts until just colouring. Add the spinach and garlic and cook quickly, turning the spinach until it has just wilted.

4 Add the raisins and season lightly with salt and pepper. Transfer to a warmed dish. Sprinkle with the croûtons and serve immediately.

Nutritional information per portion: Energy 206kcal/855kJ; Protein 5.8g; Carbohydrate 15.5g, of which sugars 11.1g; Fat 13.8g, of which saturates 1.6g; Cholesterol 0mg; Calcium 228mg; Fibre 3.4g; Sodium 218mg.

Menestra

This vegetable dish, which contains an assortment of young, new vegetables, is generally eaten to celebrate the arrival of spring.

SERVES 6

15ml/1 tbsp olive oil
115g/4oz streaky (fatty) bacon lardons or diced pancetta
1 onion, chopped
3 garlic cloves, finely chopped
90ml/6 tbsp chopped fresh parsley
175ml/6fl oz/3/4 cup dry white wine
150g/5oz green beans
200g/7oz bunched young carrots
6 small new potatoes, scrubbed
300ml/10fl oz/11/4 cups chicken stock
1 corn cob, kernels removed (optional)
200g/7oz/2 cups peas
50g/2oz mangetouts (snow peas)
salt and ground black pepper
2 hard-boiled eggs, chopped, to garnish

Directions

1 Heat the oil in a large, heavy pan and fry the bacon or pancetta over a gentle heat for about 5 minutes, or until it crisps. Remove with a slotted spoon and

reserve. Add the onion to the pan and cook in the bacon fat until softened, adding the garlic towards the end.

2 Remove the cooked onion to a food processor, add 30ml/2 tbsp of the chopped parsley and purée with a little of the white wine.

3 Prepare the vegetables. Cut the beans into short lengths, and the carrots to the same size. Bring a pan of salted water to the boil and add the potatoes. Cook forabout 10 minutes. Add the carrots to the pan of potatoes, and cook for a further 5minutes.

4 Meanwhile, return the bacon to the other pan and add the stock. Put in the beans, corn kernels and peas and lay the mangetouts over the top. Half cover the pan and leave to simmer for 5–10 minutes, until the vegetables are just cooked. Drain the potatoes and carrots and add them to the pan.

5 Add the rest of the wine and the onion purée to the pan, warming the liquid and turning the vegetables gently with a wooden spoon. Check the seasoning, adding more if necessary, and serve with the juices. Garnish with chopped egg and the remaining parsley.

Nutritional information per portion: Energy 207kcal/865kJ; Protein 8.1g; Carbohydrate 23.4g, of which sugars 9.6g; Fat 7.6g, of which saturates 2.1g; Cholesterol 12mg; Calcium 68mg; Fibre 5.5g; Sodium 274mg.

Pisto Manchego

A rich-flavoured and simple summer vegetable dish, from the poorest and
hottest part of Spain, La Mancha. It may be eaten hot or as a substantial salad, with canned tuna, or hard-boiled eggs.

SERVES 4

45ml/3 tbsp olive oil
2 Spanish onions, thinly sliced
3 garlic cloves, finely chopped
3 large green (bell) peppers, seeded and chopped
3 large courgettes (zucchini), thinly sliced
5 large ripe tomatoes or 800g/13/4lb can tomatoes, with juice
60ml/4 tbsp chopped fresh parsley
2 hard-boiled eggs, chopped (optional)
30ml/2 tbsp extra virgin olive oil (if serving cold)
salt and ground black pepper

Directions

1 Heat the oil in a large, heavy pan and cook the sliced onions and garlic gently, until they are soft.
2 Add the peppers, courgettes and tomatoes. Season and cook gently over a low heat for 20 minutes to blend the flavours.

3 Stir in 30ml/2 tbsp parsley and serve hot, if wished, topped with chopped hardboiled egg, if using, and more parsley. To serve cold, check the seasoning, adding more if needed, and sprinkle with a little extra virgin olive oil before adding the parsley garnish.

Nutritional information per portion: Energy 196kcal/812kJ; Protein 6.2g; Carbohydrate 21.3g, of which sugars 18.5g; Fat 10g, of which saturates 1.6g; Cholesterol 0mg; Calcium 109mg; Fibre 6.4g; Sodium 25mg.

Lentils with Mushrooms and Anis

The plains of Castile produce lentils for the whole of Europe. Locally they are weekly fare. In this recipe, lentejas con champiñones, they are flavoured with another regional product, anis spirit.

SERVES 4

30ml/2 tbsp olive oil
1 large onion, sliced
2 garlic cloves, finely chopped
250g/9oz/3 cups brown cap (cremini) mushrooms, sliced
150g/5oz/generous 1/2 cup brown or green lentils
4 tomatoes, cut in eighths
1 bay leaf
25g/1oz/1/2 cup chopped fresh parsley
30ml/2 tbsp anis spirit or anisette
salt, paprika and black pepper

Directions

1 Heat the oil in a large, heavy pan. Add the sliced onion and fry gently over a low heat, with the garlic, until softened but not browned.
2 Add the sliced mushrooms and stir to combine with the onion and garlic.Continue cooking, stirring gently, for a couple of minutes.

3 Add the lentils, tomato wedges and bay leaf with 175ml/6fl oz/3/4 cup water. Simmer gently, covered, for 30–40 minutes until the lentils are soft, and the liquid has almost disappeared.

4 Stir in the chopped parsley and anis. Season with salt, paprika and black pepper.

Nutritional information per portion: Energy 242kcal/1018kJ; Protein 12.5g; Carbohydrate 29.8g, of which sugars 9.5g; Fat 7.2g, of which saturates 1g; Cholesterol 0mg; Calcium 83mg; Fibre 6.9g; Sodium 23mg.

Rice and Pasta

Paella – that glorious combination of saffron rice, with shellfish, chicken or rabbit – is probably the dish most commonly associated with Spain. But there are many more festival and family dishes that combine rice with vegetables. Pasta is a 500-year-old tradition, and comes in the same versatile combinations as the rice.

Artichoke Rice Cakes with Manchego

These unusual little croquetas contain artichoke in the rice mixture, and they break open to reveal a melting cheese centre. Manchego is made from sheep's milk and has a tart flavour that goes wonderfully with the delicate taste of the rice cakes.

SERVES 6

1 large globe artichoke
50g/2oz/1/4 cup butter
1 small onion, finely chopped
1 garlic clove, finely chopped
115g/4oz/2/3 cup paella rice
450ml/3/4 pint/scant 2 cups hot chicken stock
50g/2oz/2/3 cup freshly grated Parmesan cheese
150g/5oz Manchego cheese, very finely diced

45–60ml/3/4 tbsp fine corn meal
olive oil, for frying
salt and ground black pepper
fresh flat leaf parsley, to garnish

Directions

1 Remove the heart of the artichoke and chop finely.
2 Melt the butter in a pan and fry the artichoke heart, onion and garlic for 5 minutes. Add the rice and cook for 1 minute.
3 Keeping the heat fairly high, gradually add the stock, stirring until the liquid has been absorbed and the rice is cooked – this should take about 20 minutes. Season well, then stir in the Parmesan cheese. Transfer the mixture to a bowl. Cool, cover and chill for 2 hours.
4 Spoon about 15ml/1 tbsp of the mixture into the palm of one hand, flatten slightly, and place a few pieces of diced cheese in the centre. Shape the ricearound the cheese to make a small ball. Flatten slightly, then roll in the cornmeal, shaking off any excess. Repeat with the remaining mixture to make 12 rice cakes.
5 Shallow fry the rice cakes in hot olive oil for 4–5 minutes until they are crisp and golden brown. Drain the rice cakes on kitchen paper and serve hot, garnished with flat leaf parsley.

Nutritional information per portion: Energy 354kcal/1469kJ; Protein 12g; Carbohydrate 21.8g, of which sugars 0.8g; Fat 23.6g, of which saturates 12.3g; Cholesterol 50mg; Calcium 299mg; Fibre 0.5g; Sodium 331mg.

Rice Tortitas

Like miniature tortillas, these little rice pancakes are good served hot, either plain or with tomato sauce for dipping. They make an excellent scoop for any soft vegetable mixture or dip – a very Spanish way of eating.

SERVES 4

30ml/2 tbsp olive oil
115g/4oz/1 cup cooked long grain white rice
1 potato, grated
4 spring onions (scallions), thinly sliced
1 garlic clove, finely chopped
15ml/1 tbsp chopped fresh parsley
3 large (US extra large) eggs, beaten
2.5ml/1/2 tsp paprika
salt and ground black pepper

Directions

1 Heat half the olive oil in a large frying pan and stir-fry the rice, together with the potato, spring onions and garlic, over a high heat for 3 minutes until golden.
2 Put the rice and vegetable mixture into a bowl and stir in the parsley and eggs, with the paprika and plenty of salt and pepper. Mix well.
3 Heat the remaining oil in the frying pan and drop in large spoonfuls of the rice mixture, leaving space for

spreading. Cook the tortitas for 1–2 minutes on each side until golden.

4 Drain the tortitas on kitchen paper and keep hot while cooking the remaining mixture. Serve hot.

Nutritional information per portion: Energy 185kcal/776kJ; Protein 6.8g; Carbohydrate 17.6g, of which sugars 1.2g; Fat 10.4g, of which saturates 2.1g; Cholesterol 143mg; Calcium 56mg; Fibre 1.3g; Sodium 63mg.

Moors and Christians

Moros y Cristianos is made in Valencia at the annual festival celebrating an ancient victory of the Christians over the Moors. The black beans represent the latter, and the white rice the former.

SERVES 6

400g/14oz/2 cups black beans, soaked overnight
1 onion
1 carrot
1 celery stick
1 garlic clove, finely chopped
1 bay leaf
1.75l/3 pints/2 cups water
5ml/1 tsp paprika
45ml/3 tbsp olive oil
juice of 1 orange
300g/11oz/11/2 cups long grain rice
salt and cayenne pepper

FOR THE GARNISH
chopped fresh parsley
thin wedges of orange
sliced red onion

Directions

1 Put the beans in a pan with the onion, carrot, celery, garlic, bay leaf and water. Bring to the boil and cook rapidly for 10 minutes, then reduce the heat and simmer for 1 hour. Top up the water, if necessary. When the beans are almost tender, drain, discarding the vegetables and bay leaf. Return the beans to a clean pan.

2 Blend the paprika and oil with cayenne pepper to taste and stir into the beans with the orange juice. Top up with water, if necessary. Heat until barelysimmering, then cover and cook for 15 minutes until the beans are tender. Remove from the heat and allow to stand for 15 minutes. Season with salt.

3 Cook the rice until tender. Drain, then pack into moulds and leave for 10 minutes. Transfer the rice to serving plates and arrange the beans around the edges. Garnish with the parsley, orange and red onion.

Nutritional information per portion: Energy 445kcal/1875kJ; Protein 19.7g; Carbohydrate 77.8g, of which sugars 3.2g; Fat 7g, of which saturates 1.1g; Cholesterol 0mg; Calcium 68mg; Fibre 5.6g; Sodium 12mg.

Simple Rice Salad

In this quick and easy side dish, rice and a selection of freshly chopped salad vegetables are served in a well-flavoured dressing to make a pretty, colourful salad.

SERVES 6

275g/10oz/11/2 cups long grain rice
1 bunch spring onions (scallions), finely sliced
1 green (bell) pepper, seeded and finely diced
1 yellow (bell) pepper, seeded and finely diced
225g/8oz tomatoes, peeled, seeded and chopped
30ml/2 tbsp chopped fresh flat leaf parsley or coriander (cilantro)

FOR THE DRESSING
75ml/5 tbsp extra virgin olive oil
15ml/1 tbsp sherry vinegar
5ml/1 tsp strong Dijon mustard
salt and ground black pepper

Directions

1 Cook the rice in a large pan of lightly salted boiling water for 10–12 minutes, until tender but still al dente. Be careful not to overcook it.

2 Drain the rice well in a sieve (strainer), rinse thoroughly under cold running water and drain again. Leave the rice to cool completely.

3 Place the rice in a large serving bowl. Add the spring onions, peppers,
tomatoes and parsley or coriander.
4 Make the dressing. Place all the ingredients in a screw-top jar, put the lid on and shake vigorously until well mixed. Stir the dressing into the rice and check the seasoning.

Nutritional information per portion: Energy 280kcal/1166kJ; Protein 4.9g; Carbohydrate 42.3g, of which sugars 5.5g; Fat 10g, of which saturates 1.4g; Cholesterol 0mg; Calcium 40mg; Fibre 2g; Sodium 34mg.

Paella Valenciana

A world-famous mixture of the finest Spanish ingredients, Valencia's paella contains chicken, shellfish and vegetables mixed in with succulent saffron rice.

SERVES 6–8

90ml/6 tbsp white wine
450g/1lb fresh mussels, scrubbed
115g/4oz/scant 1 cup small shelled broad (fava) beans
150g/5oz green beans, cut into short lengths
90ml/6 tbsp olive oil
6 small skinless, boneless chicken breast portions, cut into large pieces
150g/5oz pork fillet, cubed
6–8 large raw prawn (shrimp) tails, deveined, or 12 smaller raw prawns
2 onions, chopped
2–3 garlic cloves, finely chopped
1 red (bell) pepper, seeded and sliced
2 ripe tomatoes, peeled, seeded and chopped
60ml/4 tbsp chopped fresh parsley
900ml/11/2 pints/33/4 cups chicken stock
pinch of saffron threads (0.25g), soaked in 30ml/2 tbsp hot water
350g/12oz/13/4 cups paella rice, washed and drained
225g/8oz frying chorizo, sliced

115g/4oz/1 cup peas
6–8 stuffed green olives, sliced
salt, paprika and black pepper

Directions

1 Heat the wine and add the mussels, discarding any that do not close whentapped. Cover and steam until opened. Reserve the liquid and mussels separately,discarding any that do not open.

2 Briefly cook the broad beans and green beans in boiling water, then drain. Pop the broad beans out of their skins.

3 Heat 45ml/3 tbsp oil in a large paella pan or wide flameproof casserole. Season the chicken with salt and paprika and fry, turning until browned on all sides. Reserve on a plate. Season the pork with salt and paprika. Add 15ml/1 tbsp oil and fry the seasoned pork until evenly browned. Reserve with the chicken. Fry the prawns briefly in the same pan, but reserve them separately.

4 Add the remaining oil to the pan and heat. Fry the onions and garlic for 3–4 minutes until golden brown. Add the red pepper, cook for 2–3 minutes, then stir in the chopped tomatoes and parsley and cook until thickened. If cooking in the oven, preheat to 190°C/375°F/Gas 5.

5 Stir the chicken stock, the reserved mussel liquid and the saffron liquid into the vegetables. Season well with salt and pepper and bring the mixture to the boil.

When the liquid is bubbling, throw in all the rice.Stir once, then add the chicken pieces, pork, prawns, beans, chorizo and peas.

6 Transfer the pan to the oven and cook for 15–18 minutes until the rice is done. Alternatively, cook over medium-high heat for about 10 minutes. Then lower the heat and start to move the pan. A big pan needs to shift every 2–3 minutes, moving the edge of the pan round over the heat, then back to the centre. Cook until the rice is done – another 10–12 minutes.

7 Arrange the mussels and olives on top. Cover with a lid (or damp dishtowel) and leave to stand for 10 minutes, until all the liquid is absorbed. Serve straight from the pan.

COOK'S TIP

Traditionally, paella is cooked outdoors on a wide bed of hot charcoal. Indoors a big heat source such as a large hotplate or an oven is needed. Without this steady heat, the pan needs to be moved to cook the rice evenly.

Nutritional information per portion: Energy 712kcal/2978kJ; Protein 69.9g; Carbohydrate 48g, of which sugars 5.8g; Fat 26.1g, of which saturates 6.4g; Cholesterol 208mg; Calcium 98mg; Fibre 3.6g; Sodium 468mg.

Seafood Paella

This is a great dish to serve on a special occasion as it looks spectacular. A bed of scented rice is the perfect way to display a selection of seafood.

SERVES 4

45ml/3 tbsp olive oil
1 Spanish onion, chopped
2 large garlic cloves, chopped
150g/5oz frying chorizo, sliced
300g/11oz small squid, cleaned
1 red (bell) pepper, cut into strips
4 tomatoes, peeled, seeded and diced, or 200g/7oz can tomatoes
500ml/17fl oz/21/4 cups chicken stock, plus a little extra
105ml/7 tbsp dry white wine
200g/7oz/1 cup paella rice
pinch of saffron threads (0.2g), crumbled
150g/5oz/generous 1 cup peas
12 large cooked prawns (shrimp), in the shell, or 8 peeled scampi (extra large shrimp)
450g/1lb fresh mussels, scrubbed
450g/1lb clams, scrubbed

4 cooked king prawns (jumbo shrimp) or scampi, in the shell
salt and ground black pepper
chopped fresh parsley and lemon wedges, to garnish

Directions

1 Heat the olive oil in a paella pan or large frying pan, add the onion and garlic and fry until translucent. Add the chorizo and fry until lightly golden.
2 Cut the bodies of the squids into rings and the tentacles into pieces. Add thesquid to the pan and sauté over a high heat for 2 minutes.
3 Stir in the pepper and tomatoes and simmer gently for 5 minutes, until the pepper is tender. Pour in the stock and wine, stir well and bring to the boil. Stir in the rice and saffron and season well. Bring the liquid back to the boil, then lower the heat and simmer for about 10 minutes.
4 Gently stir the peas, prawns or scampi, mussels and clams into the rice, then cook for a further 15–20 minutes, until the rice is tender and all the mussels and clams have opened. (Discard any that remain closed.)
5 Remove the pan from the heat and arrange the king prawns or scampi on top. Cover and leave to stand for 5 minutes. Sprinkle the paella with chopped parsley and serve from the pan, accompanied by lemon wedges.

Nutritional information per portion: Energy 585kcal/244 Protein 36.1g; Carbohydrate 60.9g, of which sugars 10.1g; Fat 20.4g, of which saturates 5.6g; Cholesterol 268mg; Calcium 132mg; Fibre 4.2g; Sodium 1055mg.

Calderete of Rice with Fish and Aioli

Cooking rice in fish stock gives it such a splendid flavour that it is often eaten on its own, served in a little cauldron and accompanied by aioli, with the fish to follow. If you prefer, the fish can be returned to the pan while the dish is still liquid, and the fish and rice eaten with the sauce.

SERVES 6

1.6kg/31/2lb mixed fish on the bone, such as snapper, bream, grey or red mullet, or bass
45ml/3 tbsp olive oil
6 garlic cloves, smashed
1 ñora chilli or 1 hot dried chilli, seeded and chopped
250g/9oz ripe tomatoes, peeled, seeded and chopped
pinch of saffron threads (0.25g)
30ml/2 tbsp dry vermouth or white wine
1 tomato, finely diced
30ml/2 tbsp chopped fresh parsley
400g/14oz/2 cups paella rice, washed
115g/4oz small unshelled shrimps
salt and ground black pepper

FOR THE STOCK
1 onion, chopped
2 garlic cloves, chopped
1 celery stick, chopped
1 carrot, chopped
1 litre/13/4 pints/4 cups water

FOR THE AIOLI
4 garlic cloves, finely chopped
2.5ml/1/2 tsp salt
5ml/1 tsp lemon juice
2 egg yolks
250ml/8fl oz/1 cup olive oil

Directions

1 Remove the heads from the fish. Working from the head end, cut the skin along the top of the back and work the fillets off the bone. Trim as needed, put the fillets on a plate and salt them lightly. Cover and place in the refrigerator until required.

2 Make the fish stock. Put the bones, heads, tails and any other remaining bits into a large pan with the onion, garlic, celery, carrot and water. Bring to the boil, then reduce the heat, cover and simmer for about 30 minutes.

3 Make the aioli. Put the garlic in a large mortar with the salt and lemon juice and reduce to a purée. Add the egg yolks and mix thoroughly. Gradually work in the oil, drop by drop at first, to make a thick, mayonnaise-like sauce.

4 Put 15ml/1 tbsp of the olive oil in a small pan and add the whole smashed garlic cloves and dried chilli pieces. Fry for a few minutes until the garlic looks roasted.

5 Add the chopped tomatoes halfway through,crumble in the saffron and cook to form a sauce. Pour the sauce into a small blender and purée until smooth.

6 Heat the remaining 30ml/2 tbsp oil in a large frying pan and fry the fish pieces until they begin to stiffen. Strain the fish stock into a jug (pitcher), then add 900ml/11/2 pints/33/4 cups stock and the tomato sauce to the fish. Cook the fish gently for a further 3–4 minutes, until slightly underdone.

7 Remove the fish pieces from the pan with a slotted spoon to a serving dish. Season lightly and sprinkle with the vermouth or wine, diced tomato and parsley. Cover with foil and keep warm.

8 Add the rice to the stock, stir, season and bring to a simmer. Cook for 18–20minutes. Before all the liquid is absorbed, stir in the shrimps. When the rice is tender, cover and turn off the heat. Stand until all the liquid is absorbed: about 5 minutes. Serve from the pan, accompanied by the aioli. When the rice course is almost finished, uncover the fish. Stir the fish juices

into the remains of the aioli, then pour over the fish. Eat on the same plates as the rice.

Nutritional information per portion: Energy 720kcal/2996kJ; Protein 31.3g; Carbohydrate 55g, of which sugars 1.8g; Fat 40.8g, of which saturates 5.6g; Cholesterol 136mg; Calcium 133mg; Fibre 0.6g; Sodium873mg.

Vegetable Rice Pot

In this arroz de verduras, fresh seasonal vegetables are cooked in slightly spiced rice. Always taste stock, and reduce it if necessary, before adding it to rice: this is your chance to change it.

SERVES 4

1 large aubergine (eggplant)
45ml/3 tbsp olive oil
2 onions, quartered and sliced
2 garlic cloves, finely chopped
1 red (bell) pepper, halved, seeded and sliced
1 yellow (bell) pepper, halved, seeded and sliced
200g/7oz fine green beans, halved
115g/4oz/11/2 cups brown cap (cremini) mushrooms, halved
300g/11oz/11/2 cups paella rice, washed and drained
1 dried chilli, seeded and crumbled
1 litre/13/4 pints/4 cups chicken stock
115g/4oz/1 cup peas
60ml/4 tbsp chopped fresh parsley
salt and ground black pepper
fresh parsley or coriander (cilantro) leaves, to garnish

Directions

1 Halve the aubergine lengthways, then cut it into slices. Spread slices out in a large colander or on a

draining board, sprinkle with salt and leave for about 30 minutes. Rinse under cold running water and pat dry with kitchen paper.

2 Heat 30ml/2 tbsp olive oil in a deep, wide frying pan or sauté pan over a high heat. Add the aubergine slices and sauté until golden, stirring occasionally, thentransfer to kitchen paper to drain.

3 Add the remaining oil to the pan and cook the onion, and garlic until soft. Addthe peppers, green beans and mushrooms and cook briefly. Add the drained rice and stir for 1–2 minutes, then stir in the aubergine. Add the chilli and seasoning. Add the stock. Add the peas and parsley and mix together.

4 Bring the mixture up to boiling point, then cover and cook over a low heat, for 20–25 minutes, checking the liquid level towards the end (the rice should absorb the liquid, but not burn). When the rice is tender, turn off the heat, cover the pan and leave to stand for 10 minutes for the remaining liquid to be absorbed. Garnish with the parsley or coriander and serve immediately.

Nutritional information per portion: Energy 454kcal/1891kJ; Protein 11.8g; Carbohydrate 78.3g, of which sugars 13.2g; Fat 10.4g, of which saturates 1.5g; Cholesterol 0mg; Calcium 98mg; Fibre 7.4g; Sodium 13mg.

Cuban-Style Rice

Arroz a la cubana, garnished with fried eggs and bananas, is popular in the Canary Islands and Catalonia. It makes an easy and substantial supper dish.

SERVES 4

3 garlic cloves
120ml/4fl oz/1/2 cup olive oil
300g/11oz/11/2 cups long grain rice
15g/1/2oz/1 tbsp butter
4 small bananas or 2 large bananas
4 large (US extra large) eggs
salt and paprika

FOR THE TOMATO SAUCE
30ml/2 tbsp olive oil
1 onion, chopped
2 garlic cloves, finely chopped
800g/1lb 12oz can tomatoes
4 thyme or oregano sprigs
ground black pepper

Directions

1 Make the tomato sauce. Heat the oil in a pan, add the onion and garlic and fry gently, stirring, until soft. Stir

in the tomatoes and thyme or oregano and simmer for 5 minutes. Add the seasoning. Remove the herbs and keep warm.

2 Put 850ml/1 pint 8fl oz/31/2 cups water in a pan with two whole garlic cloves and 15ml/1 tbsp oil. Bring to the boil, add the rice and cook for 18 minutes until it is done, and the liquid has been absorbed.

3 Heat a pan with 30ml/2 tbsp oil and gently fry one chopped garlic clove. Add the rice, stir, season well, then turn off the heat and cover the pan.

4 Heat the butter in a frying pan with 15ml/1 tbsp oil. Halve the bananas

lengthways and fry briefly on both sides. Keep them warm.

5 Add 60ml/4 tbsp oil to the pan and fry the eggs over a medium-high heat, until the edges turn golden.Season to taste with salt and paprika. Serve the rice surrounded by the tomato sauce, bananas and fried eggs.

Nutritional information per portion: Energy 668kcal/2781kJ; Protein 13.9g; Carbohydrate 76.6g, of which sugars 15.4g; Fat 34g, of which saturates 7.2g; Cholesterol 198mg; Calcium 64mg; Fibre 2.7g; Sodium 112mg.

Andrajos

This is a rich dish of hare, wine and mushrooms, flavoured with herbs and pine nuts. The name means "rags and tatters"; it was a shepherds' dish and the shepherd would have made his own simple flour and water pasta, cut into squares.

SERVES 6

800g/13/4lb hare meat and bone (the front legs and rib end)
200ml/7fl oz/scant 1 cup red wine
120–150ml/4–5fl oz/1/2–2/3 cup olive oil
150g/5oz bacon lardons, or diced pancetta
2 onions, chopped
2 large garlic cloves, finely chopped
8 baby onions, peeled
4 carrots, diced
4 chicken thighs, halved along the bone and seasoned
seasoned plain (all-purpose) flour, for dusting
350g/12oz small open-cap mushrooms
600ml/1 pint/21/2 cups stock
5ml/1 tsp dried thyme
1 bay leaf
250g/9oz dried lasagne sheets
90ml/6 tbsp chopped fresh parsley
30ml/2 tbsp pine nuts

salt and ground black pepper

Directions

1 Starting at least two days ahead, cut the hare into portions and put in a bowl. Pour over the red wine and 15ml/1 tbsp of the oil and leave to marinate in the refrigerator for at least 24 hours.

2 Heat 30ml/2 tbsp olive oil in a large, heavy pan, add the bacon or pancetta,chopped onions and garlic and fry until the onions are translucent. Halfway through add the whole baby onions and diced carrots, and continue cooking, stirring occasionally.

3 Heat 45ml/3 tbsp oil in a large frying pan and fry the seasoned chicken pieces on both sides until golden brown. Add to the onion mixture.

4 Remove the hare from the red wine marinade, reserving the liquid. Blot the meat well on kitchen paper and dredge with the seasoned flour until well coated. Add more oil to the frying pan, if necessary, and fry the meat on all sides until browned.

5 Meanwhile, reserve eight of the smallest open-cap mushrooms. Quarter the remaining mushrooms and add to the chicken mixture. Continue cooking the hare in the frying pan, stirring every now and then, until browned.

6 When the hare is ready, arrange the pieces in the pan. Pour the reserved marinade into the frying pan to deglaze it, then pour the juices into the pan.

7 Add the stock, dried thyme and bay leaf and season with salt and pepper. Cook over a low heat for 11/2 hours, until the meat is tender. Leave to cool.

8 When ready to serve, bring plenty of water to the boil in a large roasting pan with 5ml/1 tsp salt and 15ml/1 tbsp oil. Break up the lasagne sheets and spread out the pieces in the pan. Cook for 7–8 minutes until soft, moving the pieces around to prevent them from sticking.

9 Remove all the meat from the bones and return to the pan with 60ml/4 tbsp of the parsley. Bring to a simmer. Stir the drained pasta into the sauce. Heat 15ml/1 tbsp oil in a small pan and fry the reserved mushrooms, then arrange them on top. Sprinkle with the remaining parsley and the pine nuts, and serve.

Nutritional information per portion: Energy 589kcal/2464kJ; Protein 42.4g; Carbohydrate 38g, of whichsugars 7g; Fat 28.3g, of which saturates 6.2g; Cholesterol 152mg; Calcium 75mg; Fibre 3.5g; Sodium430mg.

San Esteban Canelones

Catalans are fond of pasta, and canelones are traditional on San Esteban, the day after Christmas Day. Try to keep all the chopped stuffing ingredients the same size – small dice.

SERVES 4–8

60ml/4 tbsp olive oil
1 onion, finely chopped
1 carrot, finely chopped
2 garlic cloves, finely chopped
2 ripe tomatoes, peeled and finely chopped
25g/1oz/2 tbsp butter
150g/5oz raw chicken livers or cooked stuffing, diced
150g/5oz raw pork or cooked ham, gammon or sausage, diced
250g/9oz raw or cooked chicken, diced
5ml/1 tsp fresh thyme leaves
30ml/2 tbsp brandy
90ml/6 tbsp crème fraîche or double (heavy) cream
16 no pre-cook cannelloni tubes
75g/3oz/1 cup freshly grated Parmesan cheese
salt and ground black pepper
green salad, to serve

FOR THE WHITE SAUCE
50g/2oz/1/4 cup butter

50g/2oz/1/2 cup plain (all-purpose) flour
900ml/11/2 pints/33/4 cups milk
freshly grated nutmeg, to taste

Directions

1 Heat the oil in a large frying pan, add the onion, carrot, garlic and tomatoes and cook over a low heat, stirring, for about 10 minutes or until very soft.
2 Add the butter, then the raw meat, to the pan and cook until coloured. Add the remaining meats and sprinkle first with thyme, then with the brandy. Stir, then warm through and reduce the liquid.
3 Pour in the crème fraîche or cream, season to taste and leave to simmer for about 10 minutes. Cool briefly.
4 Preheat the oven to 190°C/375°F/Gas 5. Melt the butter in a pan, add the flour and cook, stirring, for 1–2 minutes. Gradually stir in the milk, a little at a time. Bring to simmering point, stirring until the sauce is smooth. Grate in nutmeg to taste, then season with plenty of salt and black pepper.
5 Spoon a little of the white sauce into a baking dish. Fill the cannelloni tubes with the meat mixture and arrange in a single layer in the dish. Pour the remaining white sauce over them, then sprinkle with the Parmesan cheese. Bake in the oven for 35–40 minutes, or until the pasta is tender. Leave for 10 minutes before serving with green salad.

Nutritional information per portion: Energy 480kcal/2014kJ; Protein 27.4g; Carbohydrate 40.5g, of which sugars 8.9g; Fat 23.5g, of which saturates 11.4g; Cholesterol 148mg; Calcium 282mg; Fibre 1.9g; Sodium473mg.

Fish and Shellfish

Fish and shellfish are one of the glories of Spanish cooking, largely because Spain is bordered by the Mediterranean and the Atlantic and has some of the best fishing in the world. In this chapter, you'll find a selection of appetizers, salads and main courses, including whole baked fish in simple sauces and chargrilled squid.

Seafood Salad

Ensalada de Mariscos is a very pretty arrangement of fresh mussels, prawns and squid rings served on a colourful bed of salad vegetables. In Spain, canned albacore tuna is also often included in this type of simple salad.

SERVES 6

115g/4oz prepared squid rings
12 fresh mussels, scrubbed and beards removed
1 large carrot
6 crisp lettuce leaves
10cm/4in piece cucumber, finely diced
115g/4oz cooked, peeled prawns (shrimp)
15ml/1 tbsp drained pickled capers

FOR THE DRESSING
30ml/2 tbsp freshly squeezed lemon juice
45ml/3 tbsp extra virgin olive oil
15ml/1 tbsp chopped fresh parsley
salt and ground black pepper

Directions

1 Put the squid rings into a metal sieve or vegetable steamer. Place the sieve or steamer over a pan of simmering water, cover with a lid and steam the squid for 2–3 minutes until it just turns white. Cool quickly under cold running water to prevent further cooking and drain thoroughly on kitchen paper.

2 Discard any open mussels that do not close when tapped. Cover the base of a large pan with water, add the mussels, then cover and steam for a few minutes until they open. Discard any that remain shut. Leave to cool.

3 Using a swivel-style vegetable peeler, cut the carrot into wafer-thin ribbons.Tear the lettuce into pieces and arrange on a serving plate. Add the carrot ribbons on top of the lettuce, then sprinkle over the diced cucumber.

4 Arrange the mussels, prawns and squid rings over the salad and sprinkle the capers over the top.

5 Make the dressing. Put all the ingredients in a bowl and whisk well to

combine. Drizzle over the salad. Serve at room temperature.

Nutritional information per portion: Energy 100kcal/415kJ; Protein 8.1g; Carbohydrate 2.6g, of which sugars 2g; Fat 6.4g, of which saturates 1g; Cholesterol 85mg; Calcium 50mg; Fibre 1.1g; Sodium 95mg.

Potato, Mussel and Watercress Salad

The mussels found on the Galician coast are the best in the world. The Galicians are also very proud of their potatoes and their watercress. In ensalada de mejillones, patatas y berros a creamy, well-flavoured dressing enhances all these ingredients.

SERVES 4

675g/11/2lb salad potatoes
1kg/21/4lb mussels, scrubbed and beards removed
200ml/7fl oz/scant 1 cup dry white wine
15g/1/2oz fresh flat leaf parsley, chopped
1 bunch of watercress or rocket (arugula)
salt and ground black pepper
chopped fresh chives or spring onion (scallion) tops, to garnish

FOR THE DRESSING
105ml/7 tbsp olive oil
15–30ml/1–2 tbsp white wine vinegar
5ml/1 tsp strong Dijon mustard
1 large shallot, very finely chopped
15ml/1 tbsp chopped fresh chives
45ml/3 tbsp double (heavy) cream
pinch of caster (superfine) sugar (optional)

Directions

1 Cook the potatoes in salted boiling water for 15–20 minutes, or until tender. Drain, cool, then peel. Slice into a bowl and toss with 30ml/2 tbsp of the oil for the dressing.

2 Discard any open mussels. Bring the white wine to the boil in a large, heavy pan. Add the mussels, cover and boil vigorously, shaking the pan occasionally, for 3–4 minutes, until the mussels have opened. Discard any that do not open. Drain and shell the mussels, reserving the cooking liquid.

3 Boil the reserved mussel cooking liquid until reduced to about 45ml/3 tbsp. Strain through a fine sieve over the potatoes and toss to mix.

4 To make the dressing, whisk together the remaining oil, 15ml/1 tbsp of the vinegar, the mustard, shallot and chives. Add the cream and whisk again. Adjust the seasoning, adding a little more vinegar and/or sugar to taste.

5 Toss the mussels with the potatoes, then mix in the dressing and chopped parsley. Arrange the watercress or rocket on a serving platter and top with the salad. Serve sprinkled with extra chives or a little spring onion.

Nutritional information per portion: Energy 459kcal/1918kJ; Protein 17.2g; Carbohydrate 29.2g, of which sugars 3.8g; Fat 27.7g, of which saturates 7g; Cholesterol 45mg; Calcium 222mg; Fibre 2.5g; Sodium231mg.

Surtido De Pescado

The Spanish enjoy and make the most of preserved fish. This is a very pretty dish, which uses whatever fish is available at the time, and is an ideal lastminute party appetizer.

SERVES 4

6 eggs
cos or romaine lettuce leaves
75–90ml/5–6 tbsp mayonnaise
90g/31/2oz jar Avruga herring roe, Eurocaviar grey mullet roe or undyed
(or black) lumpfish roe
2 × 115g/4oz cans sardines in oil
2 × 115g/4oz cans mackerel fillets in oil
2 × 150g/5oz jars cockles (small clams) in brine, drained
2 × 115g/4oz cans mussels or scallops in tomato sauce
fresh flat leaf parsley or dill sprigs, to garnish

Directions

1 Put the eggs in a pan with enough water to cover and bring to the boil. Turn down the heat and simmer for 10 minutes. Drain, then cover with cold water and set aside until completely cool. Peel the eggs and slice in half.

2 Arrange the lettuce leaves on a large serving platter, with the tips pointing outwards. (You may need to break off the bottom end of each leaf if the leaves are large.)
3 Place a teaspoonful or so of mayonnaise on the flat side of each halved egg and top with a spoonful of fish caviar. Carefully arrange in the centre of the dish.
4 Arrange the sardines and mackerel fillets at four points on the plate. Spoon the pickled cockles into two of the gaps, opposite each other, and the mussels in sauce in the remaining gaps. Garnish with parsley sprigs or dill. Chill untilneeded.

Nutritional information per portion: Energy 622kcal/2588kJ; Protein 56.1g; Carbohydrate 2.7g, of which sugars 0.7g; Fat 43.2g, of which saturates 8.8g; Cholesterol 482mg; Calcium 373mg; Fibre 0.2g; Sodium 661mg.

Fried Whitebait with Sherry Salsa

Small freshly fried fish are good for a tasty starter or a snack. Black-backed anchovies are the best, but need to be cooked within a day of catching. Serve the fish with lemon wedges.

SERVES 4

225g/8oz whitebait
30ml/2 tbsp seasoned plain (all-purpose) flour
60ml/4 tbsp olive oil
60ml/4 tbsp sunflower oil

FOR THE SALSA
1 shallot, finely chopped
2 garlic cloves, finely chopped
4 ripe tomatoes, roughly chopped
1 small red chilli, seeded and chopped
30ml/2 tbsp olive oil
60ml/4 tbsp sweet oloroso sherry
30–45ml/2–3 tbsp chopped mixed fresh herbs, such as parsley or basil
25g/1oz/1/2 cup stale white breadcrumbs
salt and ground black pepper

Directions

1 To make the salsa, place the chopped shallot, garlic, tomatoes, chilli and olive oil in a pan. Cover with a lid and cook gently for about 10 minutes.
2 Pour the sherry into the pan and season with the salt and black pepper to taste. Stir in the herbs and breadcrumbs, then cover and keep the salsa hot until the whitebait are ready.
3 Preheat the oven to 150°C/300°F/Gas 2. Wash the whitebait thoroughly, drain well and dry on kitchen paper, then dust in the seasoned flour.
4 Heat the oils together in a heavy frying pan and cook the fish in batches untilcrisp and golden. Drain on kitchen paper and keep warm until all the fish are cooked. Serve at once with the salsa.

Nutritional information per portion: Energy 407kcal/1689kJ; Protein 13g; Carbohydrate 13.1g, of which sugars 5.1g; Fat 32.8g, of which saturates 3.4g; Cholesterol 0mg; Calcium 526mg; Fibre 2g; Sodium 191mg.

Salt Cod Fritters with Aioli

Bacalao – salt cod – is one of the great Spanish delights, adding flavour to bland ingredients such as potatoes. If you are unfamiliar with it, then this is a delightful way to try it out. Bitesize fish cakes, dipped into rich, creamy, garlicky aioli, are irresistible as a tapas dish or appetizer.

SERVES 6

450g/1lb salt cod
500g/11/4lb floury potatoes
300ml/1/2 pint/11/4 cups milk
6 spring onions (scallions), finely chopped
30ml/2 tbsp extra virgin olive oil
30ml/2 tbsp chopped fresh parsley
juice of 1/2 lemon
2 eggs, beaten
plain (all-purpose) flour, for dusting
90g/31/2oz/11/4 cups dried white breadcrumbs
olive oil, for shallow frying
salt and ground black pepper
lemon wedges and salad leaves, to serve

FOR THE AIOLI
2 large garlic cloves, finely chopped
2 egg yolks

300ml/1/2 pint/11/4 cups olive oil
juice of 1/2 lemon, to taste

Directions

1 Soak the salt cod in cold water for at least 24 hours, changing the water two or three times. The cod should swell as it rehydrates. Sample a tiny piece. It should not taste unpleasantly salty when fully rehydrated. Drain well and pat dry with kitchen paper.

2 Cook the potatoes, unpeeled, in a pan of lightly salted boiling water for about 20 minutes, until tender. Drain. As soon as they are cool enough to handle, peel the potatoes, then mash with a fork or use a potato masher.

3 Pour the milk into a pan, add half the spring onions and simmer. Add the
soaked cod and poach gently for 10–15 minutes, until it flakes easily. Remove the cod and flake it with a fork into a bowl, discarding bones and skin.

4 Add 60ml/4 tbsp mashed potato to the cod and beat them together with a wooden spoon. Work in the olive oil, then gradually add the remaining mashed potato. Beat in the remaining spring onions and the parsley.

5 Season with lemon juice and pepper to taste – the mixture may also need a little salt but taste it before adding any. Add one beaten egg to the mixture and beat in until thoroughly combined, then chill until firm.

6 Shape the chilled fish mixture into 12–18 balls, then gently flatten into small round cakes. Coat each one in flour, then dip in the remaining beaten egg and coat with dried breadcrumbs. Chill until ready to fry.

7 Meanwhile, make the aioli. Place the garlic and a good pinch of salt in a mortar and pound to a paste with a pestle. Using a small whisk or a wooden spoon, gradually work in the egg yolks.

8 Beat in about half the olive oil, a drop at a time. When the sauce is as thick as soft butter, beat in 5–10ml/1–2 tsp lemon juice. Continue adding oil until the aioli is very thick. Season to taste, adding more lemon juice if you wish.

9 Heat about 2cm/3/4in oil in a large frying pan. Add the fritters and cook over a medium-high heat for about 4 minutes. Turn them over and cook for a further 4 minutes on the other side, until crisp and golden. Drain on kitchen paper, thenserve with the aioli, lemon wedges and salad leaves.

Nutritional information per portion: Energy 653kcal/2721kJ; Protein 32.7g; Carbohydrate 28.1g, of which sugars 4.2g; Fat 46.4g, of which saturates 7.6g; Cholesterol 178mg; Calcium 123mg; Fibre 1.4g; Sodium472mg.

Sardines En Escabeche

The Arabs invented marinades as a means of preserving meat, and escabeche means "acid" in Arabic. The fish are always fried first and then stored in vinegar.

SERVES 2–4

12–16 sardines, cleaned
seasoned plain (all-purpose) flour
30ml/2 tbsp olive oil
roasted red onion, green (bell) pepper and tomatoes, to garnish

FOR THE MARINADE
90ml/6 tbsp olive oil
1 onion, sliced
1 garlic clove, crushed
3–4 bay leaves
2 cloves
1 dried red chilli, seeded and chopped
5ml/1 tsp paprika
120ml/4fl oz/1/2 cup wine vinegar or sherry vinegar
120ml/4fl oz/1/2 cup white wine
salt and ground black pepper

Directions

1 Using a sharp knife, cut the heads off the sardines and split each of them along the belly. Turn the fish over so that the backbone is uppermost. Press down along the backbone to loosen it, then carefully lift out the backbone and as many of the remaining little bones as possible. Close the sardines up and dust them with the flour.

2 Heat the olive oil in a frying pan and fry the sardines for 2–3 minutes on each side. With a metal spatula, remove the fish to a plate and allow to cool, then pack them in a single layer in a large, shallow non-metallic dish.

3 To make the marinade, add the olive oil to the oil remaining in the frying pan. Fry the onion and garlic gently for 5–10 minutes until soft and translucent, stirring occasionally. Add the bay leaves, cloves, chilli and paprika, with pepper to taste. Fry, stirring frequently, for another 1–2 minutes.

4 Stir in the vinegar, wine and a little salt. Allow to bubble up, then pour over the sardines. The marinade should cover the fish completely. When the fish is cool, cover and chill overnight or for up to three days. Serve the sardines and their marinade, garnished with the onion, pepper and tomatoes.

Nutritional information per portion: Energy 242kcal/1004kJ; Protein 15.8g; Carbohydrate 1.7g, of which sugars 0.9g; Fat 18.1g, of which saturates 3.6g; Cholesterol 0mg; Calcium 70mg; Fibre 0.2g; Sodium 92mg.

Truchas A La Navarra

Traditionally, the trout would have come from mountain streams and been stuffed and wrapped in locally cured ham. One of the beauties of this method is that the skins come off in one piece.

SERVES 4

4 brown or rainbow trout, about 250g/9oz each, cleaned
16 thin slices Serrano ham, about 200g/7oz
50g/2oz/1/4 cup melted butter, plus extra for greasing
salt and ground black pepper
buttered potatoes, to serve (optional)

Directions

1 Extend the belly cavity of each trout, cutting up one side of the backbone. Slip a knife behind the rib bones to loosen them (sometimes just flexing the fish makes them pop up). Snip these off from both sides with scissors, and season the fish well inside.
2 Preheat the grill (broiler) to high, with a shelf in the top position. Line a baking tray with foil and butter it.
3 Working with the fish on the foil, fold a piece of ham into each belly. Use smaller or broken bits of ham for this, and reserve the eight best slices.

4 Brush each trout with a little butter, seasoning the outside lightly with salt and pepper. Wrap two ham slices round each one, crossways, tucking the ends into the belly. Grill (broil) the trout for 4 minutes, then carefully turn them over with a metal spatula, rolling them across on the belly, so the ham doesn't come loose, and grill for a further 4 minutes.

5 Serve the trout very hot, with any spare butter spooned over the top. Diners should open the trout on their plates, and eat them from the inside.

Nutritional information per portion: Energy 369kcal/1546kJ; Protein 48g; Carbohydrate 0.6g, of whichsugars 0.6g; Fat 19.4g, of which saturates 8.8g; Cholesterol 216mg; Calcium 66mg; Fibre 0g; Sodium 821mg.

Baked Trout with Rice, Tomatoes and Nuts

Trout is very popular in Spain, particularly in the north. Here is a modern recipe for trucha rellena, baked in foil with a rice stuffing in which sun-dried tomatoes are used instead of chillies.

SERVES 4

2 trout, about 500g/11/4lb each
75g/3oz/3/4 cup mixed unsalted almonds, pine nuts or hazelnuts
25ml/11/2 tbsp olive oil, plus extra for drizzling
1 small onion, finely chopped
10ml/2 tsp grated fresh root ginger
175g/6oz/11/2 cups cooked white long grain rice
4 tomatoes, peeled and very finely chopped
4 sun-dried tomatoes in oil, drained and chopped
30ml/2 tbsp chopped fresh tarragon
2 fresh tarragon sprigs
salt and ground black pepper
dressed green salad leaves, to serve

Directions

1 Preheat the oven to 190°C/375°F/Gas 5. If the trout is unfilleted, use a sharp knife to fillet it. Remove any tiny bones remaining in the cavity using a pair of tweezers.

2 Spread out the nuts in a baking tray and bake for 3–4 minutes until golden brown, shaking the tray occasionally. Chop the nuts roughly.

3 Heat the olive oil in a small frying pan and fry the onion for 3–4 minutes until soft and translucent. Stir in the grated ginger, cook for a further 1 minute, then spoon into a mixing bowl. Stir the rice, chopped and sun-dried tomatoes, toasted nuts and tarragon into the onion mixture. Season well.

4 Place the trout on individual large pieces of oiled foil and spoon the stuffinginto the cavities. Add a sprig of tarragon and a drizzle of olive oil or oil from the sun-dried tomatoes.

5 Fold the foil over to enclose each trout completely, and put the parcels in a large roasting pan. Bake for about 20 minutes or until the fish is just tender. Cut the fish into thick slices. Serve with the salad leaves.

Nutritional information per portion: Energy 458kcal/1920kJ; Protein 45.1g; Carbohydrate 19.4g, of which sugars 5g; Fat 22.8g, of which saturates 3.4g; Cholesterol 160mg; Calcium 146mg; Fibre 3.2g; Sodium 161mg.

Grilled Red Mullet with Bay Leaves

Red mullet are called salmonetes – little salmon – in Spain because of their delicate, pale pink colour. They are simple to cook on a barbecue, with bay leaves and a dribble of tangy dressing.

SERVES 4

4 red mullet, about 225–275g/8–10oz each, cleaned and descaled if
cooking under a grill (broiler)
olive oil, for brushing
fresh herb sprigs, such as fennel, dill, parsley, or thyme
2–3 dozen fresh or dried bay leaves

FOR THE DRESSING
90ml/6 tbsp olive oil
6 garlic cloves, finely chopped
1/2 dried chilli, seeded and chopped
juice of 1/2 lemon
15ml/1 tbsp parsley

Directions

1 Prepare the barbecue or preheat the grill (broiler) with the shelf 15cm/6in from the heat source.
2 Brush each fish with oil and stuff the cavities with the herb sprigs. Brush the grill pan with oil and lay bay

leaves across the cooking rack. Place the fish on top of the leaves and cook for 15–20 minutes until cooked through, turning once.

3 To make the dressing, heat the olive oil in a small pan and fry the chopped garlic with the dried chilli. Add the lemon juice and strain the dressing into a small jug (pitcher). Add the chopped parsley and stir to combine.

4 Place the mullet on warmed plates, drizzled with the dressing, and serve.

Nutritional information per portion: Energy 295kcal/1226kJ; Protein 24.3g; Carbohydrate 0.5g, of which sugars 0.1g; Fat 21.8g, of which saturates 2.4g; Cholesterol 0mg; Calcium 98mg; Fibre 0.3g; Sodium 126mg.

Mackerel in Samfaina

Samfaina is a sauce from the east coast of Spain and the Costa Brava. It is rather like a chunky vegetable stew and offsets the richness of the mackerel.

SERVES 4

2 large mackerel, filleted, or 4 fillets
plain (all-purpose) flour, for dusting
30ml/2 tbsp olive oil
lemon wedges, to serve

FOR THE SAMFAINA SAUCE
1 large aubergine (eggplant)
60ml/4 tbsp olive oil
1 large onion, chopped
2 garlic cloves, finely chopped
1 large courgette (zucchini), sliced
1 red and 1 green (bell) pepper, seeded and cut into squares
800g/13/4lb ripe tomatoes, chopped
1 bay leaf
salt and ground black pepper

Directions

1 Make the sauce. Peel the aubergine, then cut the flesh into cubes, sprinkle with salt and leave to stand in a colander for 30 minutes.

2 Heat half the oil in large, heavy pan. Fry the onion over a medium heat until it colours. Add the garlic, then the courgette and peppers and stir-fry. Add the tomatoes and bay leaf, partially cover and simmer over the lowest heat, letting the tomatoes just soften.

3 Rinse off the salt from the aubergine. Using three layers of kitchen paper, squeeze the aubergine cubes dry. Heat the remaining oil in a frying pan untilsmoking. Add the aubergine cubes a handful at a time, stirring and cooking overa high heat until brown all over. Stir into the tomato sauce.

4 Cut each mackerel into three pieces, and dust the filleted side with flour. Heat the oil in a frying pan over a high heat and put the fish in, floured side down. Fry for 3 minutes until golden. Turn and cook for another 1 minute, then slip the fish into the sauce and simmer, covered, for 5 minutes. Adjust the seasonings before serving.

Nutritional information per portion: Energy 621kcal/2591kJ; Protein 34.3g; Carbohydrate 32.4g, of which sugars 29.4g; Fat 40.6g, of which saturates 7.6g; Cholesterol 66mg; Calcium 134mg; Fibre 19.4g; Sodium 111mg.

Fried Sole with Lemon and Capers

Flat fish of different sorts abound in the Mediterranean and are usually fried simply and served with lemon wedges to squeeze over the top. Intensely flavoured capers, which grow extensively in the Balearic Islands, make a tangy addition.

SERVES 2

30–45ml/2–3 tbsp plain (all-purpose) flour
4 sole, plaice or flounder fillets, or 2 whole small flat fish
45ml/3 tbsp olive oil
25g/1oz/2 tbsp butter
60ml/4 tbsp lemon juice
30ml/2 tbsp pickled capers, drained
salt and ground black pepper
fresh flat leaf parsley, to garnish
lemon wedges, to serve

Directions

1 Sift the flour on to a plate and season well with salt and ground black pepper. Dip the fish fillets into the flour, to coat evenly on both sides.

2 Heat the oil and butter in a large frying pan until foaming. Add the fish fillets and fry over a medium heat for 2–3 minutes on each side.

3 Lift out the fillets carefully with a metal spatula and place them on a warmed serving platter. Season with salt and ground black pepper.
4 Add the lemon juice and capers to the pan, heat through and pour over the fish. Garnish with parsley, then serve with the lemon wedges.

COOK'S TIP

This is a flavourful, and quick, way to serve the fillets of any white fish. The delicate flavour is enhanced by the tangy lemon juice and capers.

Nutritional information per portion: Energy 425kcal/1773kJ; Protein 34.2g; Carbohydrate 5.9g, of whichsugars 0.2g; Fat 29.7g, of which saturates 9.3g; Cholesterol 111mg; Calcium 103mg; Fibre 0.3g; Sodium 316mg.

Sea Bass in a Salt Crust

Baking fish in a salt crust enhances the flavour and brings out the taste of the sea. In Spain, the gilthead bream is the fish most often used, but any firm fish can be cooked in this way.

SERVES 4–6

1 sea bass, about 1kg/21/4lb, gutted and scaled
1 sprig each of fresh fennel, rosemary and thyme
mixed peppercorns
2kg/41/2lb coarse sea salt
seaweed or samphire, to garnish (optional)
lemon slices, to serve

Directions

1 Preheat the oven to 240°C/475°F/Gas 9. Fill the cavity of the sea bass with the fennel, rosemary and thyme and grind over some of the mixed peppercorns.
2 Spread half the salt in a shallow baking tray and lay the sea bass on it.
3 Cover the fish all over with a 1cm/1/2in layer of salt, pressing it down firmly. Bake for 30 minutes, until the salt coagulates and is beginning to colour.
4 To serve, leave the fish on the baking tray and garnish with seaweed or

samphire, if using. Bring the fish to the table in its salt crust. Use a sharp knife to break open the crust so that the glorious aromas are released.

Nutritional information per portion: Energy 117kcal/491kJ; Protein 22.5g; Carbohydrate 0g, of which sugars 0g; Fat 2.9g, of which saturates 0.5g; Cholesterol 93mg; Calcium 152mg; Fibre 0g; Sodium 736mg.

Monkfish with Pimiento and Cream Sauce

This recipe comes from Rioja country, where a special horned red pepper is used to make a spicy sauce. Here, red peppers are used with a little chilli while cream makes a mellow pink sauce.

SERVES 4

2 large red (bell) peppers
1kg/21/4lb monkfish tail or 900g/2lb halibut
plain (all-purpose) flour, for dusting
30ml/2 tbsp olive oil
25g/1oz/2 tbsp butter
120ml/4fl oz/1/2 cup white Rioja or dry vermouth
1/2 dried chilli, seeded and chopped
8 raw prawns (shrimp), in the shell
150ml/1/4 pint/2/3 cup double (heavy) cream
salt and ground black pepper
fresh flat leaf parsley, to garnish

Directions

1 Preheat the grill (broiler) to high and cook the peppers for 8–12 minutes, turning occasionally, until they are soft, and the skins blackened. Leave to cool slightly. Skin and discard the stalks and seeds. Put the flesh into a blender, strain in the juices and purée.
2 Cut the fish into 8 steaks. Season well and dust with flour.

3 Heat the oil and butter in a frying pan and fry the fish for 3 minutes on each side. Lift out and keep warm.
4 Add the wine or vermouth and chilli to the pan and stir to deglaze the pan. Add the prawns and cook briefly, then lift out and reserve.
5 Boil the sauce to reduce by half, then strain into a small jug (pitcher). Add the cream to the pan and boil briefly to reduce.
6 Return the sauce to the pan, stir in the peppers and adjust seasoning. Pour thesauce over the fish and serve garnished with the cooked prawns and parsley.

Nutritional information per portion: Energy 500kcal/2087kJ; Protein 49.7g; Carbohydrate 7.2g, of which sugars 6.9g; Fat 27.1g, of which saturates 13.7g; Cholesterol 140mg; Calcium 70mg; Fibre 1.4g; Sodium113mg.

Vieiras De Santiago

Scallops are the symbol of St James (Santiago), and this dish is associated with his shrine at Santiago de Compostela. The scallops are covered in tomato sauce and are served in the shell.

SERVES 4

30ml/2 tbsp olive oil
1 onion, finely chopped
2 garlic cloves, finely chopped
200g/7oz can tomatoes
pinch of cayenne pepper
45ml/3 tbsp finely chopped fresh parsley
50ml/2fl oz/1/4 cup orange juice
50g/2oz/4 tbsp butter
450g/1lb large shelled scallops, or 8–12 large ones on the shell, detached
and cleaned
30ml/2 tbsp anis spirit, such as Ricard or Pernod
90ml/6 tbsp stale breadcrumbs
salt and ground black pepper

Directions

1 Heat the oil in a pan and fry the onion and garlic over a gentle heat. Add the tomatoes and cook for 10–15 minutes, stirring occasionally. Season with a little salt and cayenne pepper. Transfer to a food processor or

blender, add 30ml/2 tbsp of the parsley and the orange juice and blend to form a purée.

2 Preheat the grill (broiler) with the shelf at its highest. Arrange four curved scallop shells, or flameproof ramekin dishes, on a baking tray. Heat 25g/1oz/2 tbsp of the butter in a small frying pan and fry the scallops gently, for about 2 minutes, or until sealed but not totally cooked through.

3 Pour the anis into a ladle and set light to it. Pour over the scallops and shake the pan gently until the flames die down. Divide the scallops among the shells and salt them lightly. Add the pan juices to the tomato sauce.

4 Pour the tomato sauce over the scallops. Mix together the breadcrumbs and the remaining parsley, season very lightly and sprinkle over the top. Melt the remaining butter in a small pan and drizzle over the breadcrumbs. Grill (broil) the scallops for about 1 minute to heat through. Serve immediately.

Nutritional information per portion: Energy 394kcal/1652kJ; Protein 29.7g; Carbohydrate 25.5g, of which sugars 4.4g; Fat 18.1g, of which saturates 7.8g; Cholesterol 80mg; Calcium 95mg; Fibre 1.8g; Sodium 459mg.

Hake and Clams with Salsa Verde

Merluzaen salsa verde is a favourite Basque way of cooking hake. As they bake, the clams open up and add their delicious sea juices to the green wine and parsley sauce.

SERVES 4

4 hake steaks, about 2cm/3/4in thick
50g/2oz/1/2 cup plain (all-purpose) flour, for dusting, plus 30ml/2 tbsp
60ml/4 tbsp olive oil
15ml/1 tbsp lemon juice
1 small onion, finely chopped
4 garlic cloves, finely chopped
150ml/1/4 pint/2/3 cup fish stock
150ml/1/4 pint/2/3 cup white wine
90ml/6 tbsp chopped fresh parsley
75g/3oz/3/4 cup frozen petits pois
16 fresh clams, cleaned
salt and ground black pepper

Directions

1 Preheat the oven to 180°C/350°F/Gas 4. Season the fish, then dust with flour. Heat half the oil in a large pan, add the fish and fry for 1 minute on each side. Transfer to an ovenproof dish and sprinkle with the lemon juice.

2 Heat the remaining oil in a clean pan and fry the onion and garlic, stirring, until soft. Stir in the 30ml/2 tbsp flour and cook for about 1 minute.

3 Slowly add the stock and wine to the pan, stirring until thickened. Add 75ml/5 tbsp of the parsley and the petits pois to the sauce and season with plenty of salt and pepper.

4 Pour the sauce over the fish, and bake for 15–20 minutes, adding the clams 3–4 minutes before the end of the cooking time.

5 Discard any clams that do not open once cooked, then sprinkle the fish with the remaining parsley and serve.

Nutritional information per portion: Energy 347kcal/1449kJ; Protein 34.2g; Carbohydrate 13.2g, of which sugars 1.4g; Fat 15.2g, of which saturates 2.2g; Cholesterol 51mg; Calcium 109mg; Fibre 2.4g; Sodium 460mg.

Marmitako

This is a traditional fisherman's stew, often made at sea, with meaty tuna
steaks. The substantial fish is wonderfully balanced by sweet peppers and cider, all topped by potatoes. It takes its name from the cooking pot, known in France as a "marmite".

SERVES 4

60ml/4 tbsp olive oil
1 onion, chopped
2 garlic cloves, finely chopped
3 green (bell) peppers, seeded and chopped
1/2 dried hot chilli, seeded and chopped
4 light tuna or bonito steaks, about 150g/5oz each
400g/14oz can tomatoes with juice
10ml/2 tsp paprika
3 potatoes, diced
350ml/12fl oz/11/2 cups dry (hard) cider
salt and ground black pepper
30ml/2 tbsp chopped fresh parsley, to garnish

Directions

1 Heat half the oil in a heavy pan big enough to take the fish. Fry the onion gently until softened, then add the garlic. Add the chopped peppers and chilli and stir-fry gently.

2 Season the fish steaks. Heat the remaining oil in a frying pan and fry the fish steaks for 2 minutes on each side over a high heat. Add the tomatoes to the vegetables and stir-fry briefly. Add the paprika, then season with salt and pepper to taste.

3 Slip the fish steaks into the sauce, moving the peppers into the spaces between them. Cover with the potatoes, pushing them as flat as possible. Add the ciderand bring to a simmer. Cover and cook very gently for about 45 minutes, or untilthe potatoes are done. Check the seasoning, sprinkle with the chopped parsley and serve immediately, straight from the pan.

Nutritional information per portion: Energy 457kcal/1919kJ; Protein 39.2g; Carbohydrate 28.2g, of which sugars 16.4g; Fat 19.1g, of which saturates 3.7g; Cholesterol 42mg; Calcium 58mg; Fibre 4.4g; Sodium 100mg.

Chargrilled Squid

Calamares a la plancha are traditionally cooked on the hot griddle that is an essential part of every Spanish kitchen. The method is fast and simple and brings out the flavour of the squid.

SERVES 4

2 whole cleaned squid, with tentacles, about 275g/10oz each
75ml/5 tbsp olive oil
30ml/2 tbsp sherry vinegar
2 fresh red chillies, finely chopped
60ml/4 tbsp dry white wine
salt and ground black pepper
hot cooked rice, to serve
15–30ml/1–2 tbsp chopped parsley, to garnish

Directions

1 Make a cut down the side of the body of each squid, then open it out flat. Score the flesh on both sides of the bodies in a criss-cross pattern. Chop the tentacles into short lengths. Place all the pieces in a non-metallic dish.

2 Whisk together the oil and vinegar in a bowl. Add salt and pepper to taste, pour over the squid and toss to mix. Cover and leave to marinate for 1 hour.

3 Heat a ridged griddle pan until hot. Add the body of one of the squid and cook over a medium heat for 2–3 minutes, pressing the squid with a metal spatula to make sure it stays flat. Repeat on the other side. Cook the other squid body in the same way.

4 Cut the squid bodies into diagonal strips and arrange on the rice. Keep hot. Add the tentacles and chillies to the pan and toss over a medium heat for 2 minutes. Stir in the wine, then drizzle over the squid. Garnish with parsley.

Nutritional information per portion: Energy 258kcal/1076kJ; Protein 23.5g; Carbohydrate 2g, of which sugars 0.2g; Fat 16.4g, of which saturates 2.6g; Cholesterol 338mg; Calcium 25mg; Fibre 0g; Sodium 167mg.

Calamares Rellenos

Squid are often just stuffed with their own tentacles but, in this recipe, ham and raisins, which contrast wonderfully with the subtle flavour of the squid, are also included.

SERVES 4

2 squid, about 275g/10oz each
60ml/4 tbsp olive oil
1 small onion, finely chopped
2 garlic cloves, finely chopped
50g/2oz Serrano ham or gammon steak, diced finely
75g/3oz/scant 1/2 cup long grain rice
30ml/2 tbsp raisins, chopped
30ml/2 tbsp finely chopped fresh parsley
1/2 small (US medium) egg, beaten
plain (all-purpose) flour, for dusting
250ml/8fl oz/1 cup white wine
1 bay leaf
30ml/2 tbsp chopped fresh parsley
salt, paprika and black pepper

FOR THE TOMATO SAUCE
30ml/2 tbsp olive oil
1 onion, finely chopped
2 garlic cloves, finely chopped
200g/7oz can tomatoes

salt and cayenne pepper

Directions

1 Make the tomato sauce. Heat the oil in a heavy pan large enough to hold the squid. Gently fry the onion and garlic. Add the tomatoes and cook for 10–15 minutes. Season with salt and cayenne pepper.

2 To prepare the squid, use the tentacles to pull out the body. Cut off the tentacles, discarding the eyes and everything below. Flex the bodies to pop out the spinal structure. Chop the fin flaps and rinse the bodies well.

3 Heat half the oil in a pan and gently fry the onion and garlic together. Add the ham and squid tentacles and stir-fry. Off the heat stir in the rice, chopped raisins and parsley. Season well and add the egg to bind the ingredients.

4 Spoon the mixture into the squid bodies, then stitch each of them shut using a small skewer. Blot them with kitchen paper, then flour lightly. Heat the remaining oil in a pan and fry the squid, turning until coloured on all sides.

5 Arrange the squid in the tomato sauce. Add the wine and bay leaf. Cover the pan tightly and simmer for 30 minutes. Serve sliced into rings, surrounded by the sauce and garnished with parsley.

Nutritional information per portion: Energy 441kcal/1844kJ; Protein 28.8g; Carbohydrate 27g, of which sugars 9.4g; Fat 20.1g, of which saturates 3.2g; Cholesterol 346mg; Calcium 84mg; Fibre 2.1g; Sodium364mg.

Zarzuela

The name of this dish translates as "light musical comedy", reflecting the colour and variety of the stew, which is full of all sorts of fish and shellfish. It is distinguished from other fish stews by containing tomato as well as saffron. It's a splendid feast and not difficult to make.

SERVES 6

250g/9oz monkfish on the bone
1 gurnard, snapper or other whole white fish, about 350g/12oz, cleaned
1 sole, plaice or flounder or other whole flat fish, about 500g/11/4lb, cleaned
60ml/4 tbsp olive oil
8 small squid, with tentacles
plain (all-purpose) flour, for dusting
30ml/2 tbsp anis spirit, such as Ricard or Pernod
250ml/8fl oz/1 cup white wine
450g/1lb mussels, cleaned
4 large raw scampi (extra large shrimp), with heads
12 raw king prawns (jumbo shrimp), with heads
115g/4oz raw shelled prawns (shrimp)
salt and ground black pepper
45ml/3 tbsp chopped fresh parsley, to garnish

FOR THE STOCK
1 onion, chopped
1 celery stick, chopped
1 bay leaf

FOR THE FISH BROTH
30ml/2 tbsp oil
1 large onion, finely chopped
2 garlic cloves, finely chopped
500g/11/4lb ripe tomatoes, peeled, seeded and chopped
2 bay leaves
1 dried chilli, seeded and chopped
5ml/1 tsp paprika
pinch of saffron threads (0.2g)
salt and ground black pepper

Directions

1 Prepare the fish. Remove the flesh from the bones and cut into portions. You should have about 500g/11/4lb white fish, both firm and soft. Salt the fish and reserve on a plate in the refrigerator. (Reserve the bones and heads for making the stock.)

2 Make the stock. Put the onion, celery, bay leaf and the fish bones and heads in a pan, pour in 600ml/1 pint/21/2 cups water, and bring to the boil, then simmer for about 30minutes.

3 Make the broth in a large, heavy pan. Heat the oil and fry the onion and garlic gently until soft. Add the chopped tomatoes, bay leaves, dried chilli, paprika and crumbled saffron and cook gently to make a sauce.

4 To cook the fish and shellfish, heat the oil in a large frying pan. Put in the squid tentacles, face down, and cook for 45 seconds, to make “flowers”. Reserve on a plate.

5 Flour and fry the monkfish and white fish for 3 minutes on each side, then the flat fish for 2 minutes on each side. Cut the squid bodies into rings and fry. Pour the anis spirit into a ladle, flame it and pour over the fish remaining in the pan. Remove the fish and reserve.

6 Strain the fish stock into the tomato sauce and add the wine. Bring to a simmer. Add the mussels in two batches. Cover for a couple of minutes, then remove to a plate, discard any closed mussels, and remove the upper shells.

7 Add the scampi and cook for about 8 minutes, then lift out using a slottedspoon. Cut with scissors along the underside from the head to the tail. Add theraw king prawns for 3–4 minutes, then lift out and reserve.

8 About 20 minutes before serving, assemble the casserole. Add the seafood to the hot broth in the following order, bringing the liquid back to simmering each time: firm white fish, soft white fish (with squid rings and pan juices), large shellfish in the shell, cooked shellfish in the shell, then any small shelled

prawns.If the liquid level falls below the seafood, make it up with more wine. Check the seasonings.

9 Rearrange the soup with the best-looking shellfish and squid flowers on top. Scatter over the mussels, cover and leave to steam for 2 minutes. Garnish with parsley and serve.

Nutritional information per portion: Energy 326kcal/1367kJ; Protein 34.8g; Carbohydrate 5.4g, of which sugars 3.4g; Fat 14.4g, of which saturates 2.3g; Cholesterol 248mg; Calcium 79mg; Fibre 1g; Sodium 264mg.

Poultry, Meat and Game

From chicken in saffron rice to kidneys in sherry and the ever-popular meatballs in tomato sauce, there are dishes here for every occasion. Pork is a favourite meat, and lamb, veal, beef and rabbit are used widely. Poultry and game birds are immensely popular in Spain and may be stuffed with fruit, marinated in wine, cooked with seasonal vegetables or served in delicious sauces.

Orange Chicken Salad

With their tangy flavour, orange segments are the perfect partner for tender chicken in this tasty rice salad. To appreciate all the flavours fully, serve the salad at room temperature.

SERVES 4

3 large seedless oranges
175g/6oz/scant 1 cup long grain rice
175ml/6fl oz/3/4 cup vinaigrette
10ml/2 tsp strong Dijon mustard
2.5ml/1/2 tsp caster (superfine) sugar
450g/1lb cooked chicken, diced
45ml/3 tbsp chopped fresh chives

75g/3oz/3/4 cup almonds or cashew nuts, toasted
salt and ground black pepper
mixed salad leaves, to serve

Directions

1 Pare one of the oranges thinly, removing only the rind, not the pith. Put the pieces of orange rind in a pan and add the rice. Pour in 475ml/16fl oz/2 cups water, add a pinch of salt and bring to the boil. Cover and cook over a very low heat for 15 minutes, or until the rice is tender and the water has been absorbed.

2 Meanwhile, peel the oranges, removing all the pith. Separate them into
segments over a plate. Add the orange juice from the plate to the vinaigrette with the mustard and sugar, whisking to combine. Check the seasoning.

3 Discard the pieces of orange rind. from the cooked rice. Spoon the rice into a bowl, let it cool slightly, then add half the dressing. Toss well, then set aside to cool completely.

4 Add the chicken, chives, nuts and orange segments to the rice. Pour over theremaining dressing and toss. Serve on a bed of salad leaves.

Nutritional information per portion: Energy 642kcal/2678kJ; Protein 35.6g; Carbohydrate 49.5g, of which sugars 14g; Fat 33.7g, of which saturates 4.7g; Cholesterol 79mg; Calcium 118mg; Fibre 3.5g; Sodium278mg.

Chicken with Lemon and Garlic

Pollo con limón y ajillo is one of the simplest and most delicious ways to serve chicken. It makes a good tapas dish, served with cocktail sticks, or a supper for two, with fried potatoes.

SERVES 2–4

2 skinless chicken breast fillets
30ml/2 tbsp olive oil
1 shallot, finely chopped
4 garlic cloves, finely chopped
5ml/1 tsp paprika
juice of 1 lemon
30ml/2 tbsp chopped fresh parsley
salt and ground black pepper
fresh flat leaf parsley, to garnish
lemon wedges, to serve

Directions

1 Remove the little fillet from the back of each breast. If the breast still looks fatter than a finger, bat it with a rolling pin to make it thinner. Slice all the chicken meat into strips.

2 Heat the oil in a large frying pan. Stir-fry the chicken strips with the shallot, garlic and paprika over a high heat for about 3 minutes until cooked through.

3 Add the lemon juice and parsley and season with salt and pepper to taste. Serve hot with lemon wedges, garnished with flat leaf parsley.

Nutritional information per portion: Energy 138kcal/579kJ; Protein 18.5g; Carbohydrate 1.5g, of which sugars 1.1g; Fat 6.5g, of which saturates 1g; Cholesterol 53mg; Calcium 30mg; Fibre 0.8g; Sodium 49mg.

Crumbed Chicken with Green Mayonnaise

Pechugas de pollo rebozadas are sold ready-prepared in every butcher's in the South. Identical to schnitzel, these crispy, golden chicken breast portions show the Jewish influence on cooking in the region. Lemon wedges are a popular accompaniment.

SERVES 4

4 chicken breast fillets, each weighing about 200g/7oz
juice of 1 lemon
5ml/1 tsp paprika
plain (all-purpose) flour, for dusting
1–2 eggs
dried breadcrumbs, for coating
about 60ml/4 tbsp olive oil
salt and ground black pepper
lemon wedges, to serve (optional)

FOR THE MAYONNAISE
120ml/4fl oz/1/2 cup mayonnaise
30ml/2 tbsp pickled capers, drained and chopped
30ml/2 tbsp chopped fresh parsley

Directions

1 Start a couple of hours ahead, if you can. Skin the chicken fillets. Lay them outside down and, with a sharp knife, cut horizontally, almost through, from the

rounded side. Open them up like a book. Press gently, to make a roundish shape, the size of a side plate. Sprinkle with lemon juice and paprika.

2 Set out three plates. Sprinkle flour over one, seasoning it well. Beat the egg with a little salt and pour into the second. Sprinkle the third with dried breadcrumbs. Dip the fillets first into the flour on both sides, then into the egg, then into the breadcrumbs. Chill the crumbed chicken, if you have time.

3 Put the mayonnaise ingredients in a bowl and mix well to combine.

4 Heat the oil in a heavy frying pan over a high heat. Fry the fillets, two at a time, turning after 3 minutes, until golden on both sides. Add more oil for the second batch if needed. Serve at once, with the mayonnaise and lemon wedges, if using.

Nutritional information per portion: Energy 594kcal/2476kJ; Protein 52g; Carbohydrate 12.5g, of which sugars 1.1g; Fat 37.7g, of which saturates 6g; Cholesterol 210mg; Calcium 64mg; Fibre 1g; Sodium 372mg.

Pollo A La Española

This colourful chicken dish is made throughout Spain in an infinite number of variations. Cubed Serrano ham can replace the bacon, but the fat the latter gives off is a constant theme in the Spanish kitchen, so helps to add to its character.

SERVES 4

5ml/1 tsp paprika
4 free-range or cornfed chicken portions
45ml/3 tbsp olive oil
150g/5oz smoked bacon lardons, or diced pancetta
1 large onion, chopped
2 garlic cloves, finely chopped
1 green (bell) pepper
1 red (bell) pepper
450g/1lb tomatoes or 400g/14oz canned tomatoes
30ml/2 tbsp chopped fresh parsley
salt and ground black pepper
boiled rice, to serve (optional)

Directions

1 Rub paprika and salt into the chicken portions. Heat 30ml/2 tbsp oil in a
large frying pan. Put in the chicken portions, skin side down, and fry gently.

2 Heat 15ml/1 tbsp oil in a large, heavy pan and then add the diced bacon or pancetta. When the bacon or pancetta starts to give off fat, add the chopped onion and garlic, frying very gently until soft.

3 Remove and discard the stalks and seeds from the peppers and chop the flesh. Spoon off a little fat from the chicken pan, then add the peppers, fitting them between the chicken portions, and cook over a gentle heat.

4 When the onions are soft, stir in the tomatoes and season. Arrange the chicken pieces in the sauce, and stir in the cooked peppers.

5 Cover the pan tightly and simmer over a low heat for 15 minutes. Check the seasoning, stir in the parsley and serve with rice, if you like.

Nutritional information per portion: Energy 365kcal/1529kJ; Protein 44.1g; Carbohydrate 9.6g, of which sugars 8.6g; Fat 16.9g, of which saturates 4.2g; Cholesterol 125mg; Calcium 36mg; Fibre 2.6g; Sodium 682mg.

Arroz Con Pollo

Many Spanish families eat rice once a week, referring to it as arroz unless it is paella. This dish, rice with chicken, is cooked in one pot, with more liquid than a paella. Seasonal vegetables are included and peas and corn can be used.

SERVES 4

60ml/4 tbsp olive oil
6 chicken thighs, halved along the bone
5ml/1 tsp paprika
1 large Spanish onion, roughly chopped
2 garlic cloves, finely chopped
1 chorizo sausage, sliced
115g/4oz Serrano or cooked ham or gammon, diced
1 red (bell) pepper, seeded and roughly chopped
1 yellow (bell) pepper, seeded and roughly chopped
225g/8oz/1 generous cup paella rice, washed and drained
2 large tomatoes, chopped or 200g/7oz can chopped tomatoes
120ml/4fl oz/1/2 cup amontillado sherry
750ml/11/4 pints/3 cups chicken stock
5ml/1 tsp dried oregano or thyme
1 bay leaf
salt and ground black pepper

15 green olives and chopped fresh flat leaf parsley, to garnish

Directions

1 Heat the oil in a large, heavy pan or flameproof casserole dish. Season the chicken pieces with salt and paprika. Fry until nicely brown all over, then reserve on a plate.

2 Add the onion and garlic to the pan and fry gently until beginning to soften.Add the chorizo and ham or gammon and stir-fry. Add the chopped peppers.Cook until they begin to soften.

3 Sprinkle in the drained rice and cook, stirring, for 1–2 minutes. Add the

tomatoes, sherry, chicken stock and dried herbs and season well. Arrange the chicken pieces deep in the mixture, and tuck in the bay leaf.

4 Cover and cook over a very low heat for 30–40 minutes, until the chicken and rice are done. Stir, then garnish and serve.

Nutritional information per portion: Energy 654kcal/2736kJ; Protein 49.7g; Carbohydrate 59.3g, of which sugars 11.2g; Fat 20.6g, of which saturates 5g; Cholesterol 132mg; Calcium 52mg; Fibre 2.8g; Sodium 651mg.

Pollo Con Langostinos

Chicken with prawns is another gorgeous Catalan dish. The sauce is thickened with a picada or paste of ground toasted almonds, which is more convenient than making a roux. This special picada traditionally includes butter biscuit rather than the bread that normally goes into picada.

SERVES 4

1.3kg/3lb free-range chicken
75–90ml/5–6 tbsp olive oil
1 large onion, chopped
2 garlic cloves, finely chopped
400g/14oz tomatoes, peeled and seeded then chopped or 400g/14oz can tomatoes, drained
1 bay leaf
150ml/1/4 pint/2/3 cup dry white wine
450g/1lb large raw prawns (shrimp), or 16 large shelled prawn tails
15g/1/2oz/1 tbsp butter
30ml/2 tbsp anis spirit, such as Ricard or Pernod
75ml/21/2fl oz/1/3 cup double (heavy) cream
1.5ml/1/4 tsp cayenne pepper
salt, paprika and ground black pepper
fresh flat leaf parsley, to garnish
boiled rice or raw spinach salad, to serve

FOR THE PICADA
25g/1oz/1/4 cup blanched almonds
15g/1/2oz/1 tbsp butter
1 garlic clove, finely chopped
3 Marie, Rich Tea or plain all-butter biscuits (cookies), broken
90ml/6 tbsp chopped fresh parsley

Directions

1 Cut the chicken into eight serving portions, then separate the small fillet from the back of each breast portion. Rub salt and paprika into the chicken.
2 Heat 30ml/2 tbsp oil in a large, heavy pan and fry the onion and garlic until soft. Put in the chicken pieces, skinside down, and fry over a medium heat, turning until they are golden on all sides.
3 To make the picada, dry-fry the almonds in a frying pan, shaking it regularly, until they are coloured. Transfer them to a blender and process until smooth.
4 Add the butter to the pan and gently fry the garlic, then add it to the blender, with the broken biscuits. Reduce the biscuits to crumbs then add the chopped parsley and blend to a purée, adding a little of the wine intended for the casserole.
5 Add the tomatoes to the chicken, tuck in the bay leaf and cook down to a sauce, stirring occasionally. Pour in the remaining wine, season to taste with salt and ground black pepper, and leave to simmer gently.

6 Check the shelled prawn tails, if using: if they have a black thread along the back, nick it out with a knife. Heat 15ml/1 tbsp oil and the butter in the frying pan and add the prawns. Cook over a medium heat for 2 minutes on each side.

7 Pour the anis spirit into a ladle and set light to it. Off the heat, pour this over the prawns and let it burn off. Stir in the juices from the chicken, then transfer the contents back to the chicken pan.

8 Remove the bay leaf from the pan and stir in the picada, then the cream. Add cayenne to taste and check the seasonings, adding a little more if necessary. Heat through gently and serve garnished with parsley.

Nutritional information per portion: Energy 881kcal/3655kJ; Protein 52.5g; Carbohydrate 9.8g, of which sugars 4.1g; Fat 65.8g, of which saturates 22g; Cholesterol 368mg; Calcium 110mg; Fibre 1.7g; Sodium 934mg.

Chicken Casserole with Spiced Figs

The Catalans have a reputation for serving fruit with poultry and meat. Here pollo con higos is cooked with a beautifully spiced sauce, which goes perfectly with a Catalan Cabernet Sauvignon.

SERVES 4

50g/2oz bacon lardons or pancetta, diced
15ml/1 tbsp olive oil
1.3–1.6kg/3–31/2lb free-range or cornfed chicken, jointed into eight
pieces
120ml/4fl oz/1/2 cup white wine
finely pared rind of 1/2 lemon
50ml/2fl oz/1/4 cup chicken stock
salt and ground black pepper
green salad, to serve

FOR THE FIGS
150g/5oz/3/4 cup sugar
120ml/4fl oz/1/2 cup white wine vinegar
1 lemon slice
1 cinnamon stick
120ml/4fl oz/1/2 cup water
450g/1lb fresh figs

Directions

1 Prepare the figs. Gently simmer the sugar, vinegar, lemon and cinnamon with the water for 5 minutes. Add the figs and cook for 10 minutes. Remove from the heat and leave to stand for 3 hours.

2 Fry the bacon or pancetta in a frying pan until golden. Transfer to an ovenproof dish. Add the oil to the pan. Season the chicken, brown on both sides, then transfer to the ovenproof dish.

3 Preheat the oven to 180°C/350°F/Gas 4. Drain the figs. Add the wine andlemon rind to the pan and boil until the wine has reduced and is syrupy. Pour over the chicken.

4 Cook the chicken in the oven, uncovered, for about 20 minutes, then add the figs and chicken stock. Cover and return to the oven for a further 10 minutes. Serve with a green salad.

Nutritional information per portion: Energy 811kcal/3396kJ; Protein 44g; Carbohydrate 69.8g, of which sugars 69.8g; Fat 39.2g, of which saturates 10.9g; Cholesterol 215mg; Calcium 183mg; Fibre 4.3g; Sodium 394mg.

Chicken Chilindrón

This famous chicken dish from Navarra has a spicy red pepper sauce. In the past, the dried choricero pepper was used alone, but fresh red peppers spiced with chilli are used nowadays.

SERVES 4

675g/11/2lb red (bell) peppers
4 free-range chicken portions
10ml/2 tsp paprika
30ml/2 tbsp olive oil
1 large onion, chopped
2 garlic cloves, finely chopped
200g/7oz Serrano or other ham, in one piece, or a gammon chop, diced
200g/7oz can chopped tomatoes
1 dried guindilla or other hot dried chilli, chopped, or 2.5ml/1/2 tsp chilli
powder, to taste
salt and ground black pepper
chopped fresh parsley, to garnish
small new potatoes, to serve

Directions

1 Preheat the grill (broiler) to high. Put the peppers on a baking sheet and grill (broil) for 8–12 minutes, until the skins have blackened, turning every so often. Place

in a bowl, cover with clear film (plastic wrap) and leave to cool.

2 Rub salt and paprika into the chicken portions. Heat the oil in a large frying pan and add the chicken portions, skinside down. Fry over a medium-low heat, turning until golden on all sides.

3 Spoon 45ml/3 tbsp fat from the frying pan into a large, heavy pan. Fry the onion and garlic until soft. Add the ham or gammon, stirring occasionally, for afew minutes. Add the chopped tomatoes to the pan, with the chilli or chillipowder. Cook for 4–5 minutes, letting the sauce reduce.

4 Peel the skins off the peppers and discard these and the stalks. Put the peppers into a blender and strain in the juices, discarding the seeds. Process, then add to the pan and stir in. Heat through, then add the chicken pieces. Cook, covered, for 15 minutes and check the seasonings. Garnish with a little parsley and serve with small new potatoes.

Nutritional information per portion: Energy 332kcal/1396kJ; Protein 47.6g; Carbohydrate 13.8g, of which sugars 12.4g; Fat 10g, of which saturates 2.1g

Roast Turkey with Black Fruit Stuffing

Columbus introduced turkeys from America to Spain, and at first they were cooked like peacocks – stuffed, then roasted inside a pig's caul.

SERVES 8

3kg/61/2lb bronze or black turkey, weighed without the giblets
60ml/4 tbsp oil
200g/7oz rashers (strips) streaky (fatty) bacon

FOR THE STUFFING
30ml/2 tbsp olive oil
1 onion, chopped
2 garlic cloves, finely chopped
115g/4oz fatty bacon lardons
150g/5oz morcilla or black pudding (blood sausage), diced
1 turkey liver, diced
50g/2oz/1/2 cup Muscatel raisins, soaked in 45ml/3 tbsp anis spirit, such
as Ricard, and chopped
115g/4oz ready-to-eat pitted prunes, chopped
50g/2oz/1/2 cup almonds, chopped
1.5ml/1/4 tsp dried thyme
finely grated rind of 1 lemon
freshly grated nutmeg

60ml/4 tbsp chopped fresh parsley
1 large (US extra large) egg, beaten
60ml/4 tbsp cooked rice or stale breadcrumbs
salt and ground black pepper

FOR THE SAUCE
45ml/3 tbsp plain (all-purpose) flour
350ml/12fl oz/11/2 cups turkey giblet stock, warmed
350ml/12fl oz/11/2 cups red grape juice
30ml/2 tbsp anis spirit, such as Ricard
salt and ground black pepper

Directions

1 Make the stuffing. Heat the oil in a pan and fry the onion, garlic and bacon. Remove to a large bowl. Fry the morcilla or black pudding for 3–4 minutes and the liver for 2–3 minutes.

2 Add the soaked raisins, prunes, almonds, thyme, lemon rind, nutmeg,

seasoning and parsley. Stir in the egg and rice or breadcrumbs.

3 About 3 hours before carving, preheat the oven, with a low shelf, to

200°C/400°F/Gas 6. Remove the turkey's wishbone, running fingernails up the two sides of the neck to find it. Just nick it out. Season the turkey inside, stuff and retruss it. Season outside. Keep at room temperature.

4 Heat a roasting pan in the oven with 60ml/4 tbsp oil. Put in the turkey and baste the outside. Lay the bacon

over the breast and legs. Reduce the oven temperature to 180°C/350°F/Gas 4 and roast for 21/4–21/2 hours, basting once.

5 To test, insert a skewer into the thickest part of the inside leg. The juices should run clear. Remove the trussing thread and transfer the turkey to a heated serving plate. Keep warm.

6 Make the sauce. Skim as much fat as possible from the roasting pan. Sprinkle in the flour and cook gently for a few minutes, stirring. Stir in the warm turkey stock and bring to simmering point. Add the grape juice and anis, and bring back to simmering. Taste for seasoning. Pour into a jug (pitcher). Carve the turkey and serve with the sauce.

Nutritional information per portion: Energy 662kcal/2772kJ; Protein 66.3g; Carbohydrate 27.9g, of which sugars 15.5g; Fat 31.5g, of which saturates 8.1g; Cholesterol 274mg; Calcium 104mg; Fibre 2.2g; Sodium 658mg.

Spiced Duck with Pears

This Catalan speciality is a fabulous combination of poultry and fruit. This dish features the picada, a great Catalan invention made of pounded nuts, which both flavours and thickens the final sauce. Serve with a bottle of Gran Sangre de Toro.

SERVES 6

6 duck portions, preferably Barbary, either breast portions or leg pieces
1 large onion, thinly sliced
1 cinnamon stick, halved
4 thyme sprigs
475ml/16fl oz/2 cups duck or chicken stock
3 firm, ripe pears
30ml/2 tbsp olive oil
25g/1oz/1/4 cup raisins
salt and ground black pepper
young thyme sprigs or fresh parsley, to garnish
mashed potatoes and green vegetables, to serve (optional)

FOR THE PICADA
30ml/2 tbsp olive oil
1/2 slice stale bread, without crusts

2 garlic cloves, sliced
15g/1/2oz/12 almonds, toasted
15g/1/2oz/12 hazelnuts, toasted
15ml/1 tbsp chopped fresh parsley
salt and ground black pepper

Directions

1 Preheat the oven to 180°C/350°F/Gas 4. Season the duck portions, pricking theskins with a fork. Fry them, skinside down, for about 5 minutes, until they giveoff fat. Turn them over and fry on the other side more briefly.

2 Transfer the duck to an ovenproof dish and drain off all but 15ml/1 tbsp of the fat left in the pan.

3 Add the onion to the pan and fry for 5 minutes. Add the cinnamon, thyme and stock and bring to the boil. Pour over the duck, reserving a little of the stock, and bake for 11/4 hours.

4 Meanwhile, make the picada. Heat the olive oil in a frying pan and fry the bread over a high heat. Drain on kitchen paper and reserve. Briefly fry the garlic and reserve with the bread.

5 Put all the nuts in a mortar and pound, or reduce to a paste in a food processor or blender. Add the bread, torn into pieces, and the garlic, and reduce to a thick, smooth paste with a little pan stock. Add the parsley and seasoning.

6 Peel, core and halve the pears. Fry quickly in the oil in the frying pan until beginning to colour on the cut sides.

7 Add the picada to the ovenproof dish with the raisins and pears. Bake for a further 15 minutes until the pears are tender. Season to taste and garnish with thyme or parsley. Serve with mashed potatoes and vegetables, if you wish.

Nutritional information per portion: Energy 296kcal/1235kJ; Protein 21.5g; Carbohydrate 14.7g, of which sugars 11.3g; Fat 18.8g, of which saturates 2.8g; Cholesterol 110mg; Calcium 40mg; Fibre 2.3g; Sodium 147mg.

Guinea Fowl with Saffron and Nut Sauce

The Arabs introduced saffron to Spain and this is a Moorish sauce. Pepita is the Spanish word for a seed or nut, hence the name pintadaenpepitoria. Serve with a Rioja Reserva.

SERVES 4

25g/1oz/1/4 cup blanched almonds
pinch of saffron threads (0.1g)
120ml/4fl oz/1/2 cup chicken stock
1.2–1.3kg/21/2–3lb guinea fowl
60ml/4fl oz/1/2 cup olive oil
1 thick slice of bread, without crusts
2 garlic cloves, finely chopped
120ml/4fl oz/1/2 cup fino sherry
1 bay leaf, crumbled
4 thyme sprigs
15ml/1 tbsp finely chopped fresh parsley
pinch of freshly grated nutmeg
pinch of ground cloves
juice of 1/2 lemon
5ml/1 tsp paprika
salt and ground black pepper

Directions

1 Preheat the oven to 150°C/300°F/Gas 2. Spread the almonds on a baking sheet and toast in the oven for

about 20 minutes. Crumble the saffron into a small bowl, pour over 30ml/2 tbsp hot chicken stock and leave to soak.

2 Cut the bird into eight serving pieces, discarding the wing tips, backbone, breastbones and leg tips. This will give you two legs (split them at the joint), twowings with one-third of the breast attached, and two short breast pieces.

3 Heat the olive oil in a large, heavy pan and fry the bread slice on both sides. Fry the garlic quickly, then remove both to a blender.

4 Season the poultry well and fry them, turning until golden on all sides. Add theremaining stock and the sherry to the pan, stirring to deglaze the pan. Add the bay leaf and thyme and cover. Cook gently for 10 minutes.

5 Grind together the bread, garlic and almonds. Add the parsley, saffron liquid, nutmeg and cloves, and purée. Stir into the poultry juices, add the lemon juice and paprika, season and serve.

Nutritional information per portion: Energy 589kcal/2442kJ; Protein 38.6g; Carbohydrate 4.2g, of which sugars 0.9g; Fat 42.8g, of which saturates 10.5g; Cholesterol 192mg; Calcium 40mg; Fibre 0.6g; Sodium189mg.

Perdices Con Uvas

Partridges are Spain's commonest game birds. They have a natural affinity with grapes which are used for the garnish and sauce in this dish. Game hens or any plump small bird can also be used.

SERVES 4

4 partridges, cleaned
500g/11/4lb red grapes, split and seeded, plus extra to garnish
45–60ml/3–4 tbsp olive oil
4 rashers (slices) smoked streaky (fatty) bacon, halved across
1 onion, chopped
2 garlic cloves, finely chopped
1 bay leaf
120ml/4fl oz/1/2 cup dry white wine
250ml/8fl oz/1 cup game or chicken stock
freshly grated nutmeg
salt and ground black pepper
30ml/2 tbsp chopped fresh parsley, to garnish

Directions

1 Season the birds inside and out, then stuff with 250g/ 9oz grapes. Put 45ml/3 tbsp oil in a large, heavy pan into which the birds will fit snugly.

2 Fry the bacon until crisp, then reserve on a plate. Put the birds into the pan breast sides down and fry until coloured. Turn them with two spoons, frying and turning until brown all over. Remove.

3 Fry the onion and garlic, adding a little more oil if needed, until softened. Return the birds to the casserole and put two pieces of bacon on top of each. Push 125g/5oz grapes in round them, and add the bay leaf. Pour in the white wine and stock. Add plenty of black pepper. Simmer, covered, for 30 minutes.

4 Remove the birds and bacon to a plate. Spoon the pan contents into a foodprocessor. Discard the bay leaf, and purée. Add the nutmeg and season.

5 Return the birds to the pan, pour the sauce around them, and add 125g/5oz grapes. Heat through. Serve, garnished with extra grapes, crumbled bacon and a little parsley.

Nutritional information per portion: Energy 832kcal/3494kJ; Protein 125.6g; Carbohydrate 15.6g, of which sugars 15.6g; Fat 27.9g, of which saturates 7.6g; Cholesterol 13mg; Calcium 171mg; Fibre 0.7g; Sodium 718mg.

Braised Quail with Winter Vegetables

Quail are both plentiful and very popular in Spain, especially during the hunting season. Here, in cordonicesestofadas, they are cooked and served in a red wine sauce.

SERVES 4

4 quail, cleaned
60ml/4 tbsp olive oil
175g/6oz small carrots, cut into chunks
175g/6oz baby turnips, cut into chunks
4 shallots, halved
450ml/3/4 pint/scant 2 cups red wine
30ml/2 tbsp Spanish brandy
salt and ground black pepper
fresh flat leaf parsley, to garnish

FOR THE CROÛTES
4 slices stale bread, crusts removed
60ml/4 tbsp olive oil

Directions

1 Preheat the oven to 220°C/425°F/Gas 7. Season the quail with salt and ground black pepper.
2 Heat half the oil in a flameproof casserole and add the quail. Fry until browned all over. Remove from the casserole and set aside.

3 Add more oil to the casserole with all the vegetables and shallots. Cook until just colouring. Return the quail to the casserole, breast sides down, and add the wine. Cover and transfer to the oven. Cook for 30 minutes, or until the quail are tender.
4 Using a 10cm/4in plain cutter stamp out rounds from the bread. Heat the oil in a frying pan and cook the bread over a high heat until golden on both sides. Drain on kitchen paper and keep warm.
5 Place the croûtes on plates and set a quail on top of each. Arrange thevegetables around the quail.
6 Boil the cooking juices hard until reduced to a syrupy consistency. Add the brandy and warm through, then season. Drizzle over the quail and garnish with parsley, then serve.

Nutritional information per portion: Energy 591kcal/2456kJ; Protein 24.4g; Carbohydrate 14.3g, of which sugars 6.7g; Fat 38.8g, of which saturates 7.6g; Cholesterol 116mg; Calcium 68mg; Fibre 2.5g; Sodium 184mg.

Marinated Pigeon in Red Wine

Migrating pigeons fly over the mountains of Spain twice a year, and shooting them is a big sport. Here they are marinated in spiced vinegar and red wine, then cooked in the marinade.

SERVES 4

4 pigeons (squabs), each about 225g/8oz, cleaned
30ml/2 tbsp olive oil
1 onion, roughly chopped
225g/8oz/3 cups brown cap (cremini) mushrooms, sliced
plain (all-purpose) flour, for dusting
300ml/1/2 pint/11/4 cups beef or game stock
30ml/2 tbsp chopped fresh parsley
salt and ground black pepper
fresh flat leaf parsley, to garnish

FOR THE MARINADE
15ml/1 tbsp olive oil
1 onion, chopped
1 carrot, chopped
1 celery stick, chopped
3 garlic cloves, sliced
6 allspice berries, bruised
2 bay leaves
8 black peppercorns, bruised

120ml/4fl oz/1/2 cup red wine vinegar
150ml/1/4 pint/2/3 cup red wine

Directions

1 Starting a day ahead, combine all the ingredients for the marinade in a large dish. Add the pigeons and turn them in the marinade. Cover and chill for 12 hours. Turn occasionally.

2 Preheat the oven to 150°C/300°F/Gas 2. Heat the oil in a large, flameproof casserole and cook the onion and mushrooms for about 5 minutes, until the onion has softened.

3 Meanwhile, remove the pigeons to a plate with a slotted spoon and strain the marinade into a bowl, then set both aside separately.

4 Sprinkle the flour on the pigeons and add them to the casserole, breast sides down. Pour in the marinade and stock, and add the chopped parsley and seasoning. Cover and cook in the oven for 11/2 hours or until tender.

5 Check the seasoning, then serve the pigeons on warmed plates with the sauce. Garnish with the fresh parsley leaves.

Nutritional information per portion: Energy 286kcal/1189kJ; Protein 25.6g; Carbohydrate 1.5g, of which sugars 1g; Fat 17.4g, of which saturates 0.9g; Cholesterol 0mg; Calcium 23mg; Fibre 0.8g; Sodium 98mg.

Liver and Bacon Casserole

In Spain, liver means pig's liver, and is cooked here in a well-seasoned sauce. The pig's liver is the first thing to be eaten from the new pig, and so is associated with one of the big feasts of the year, Matanza. You can substitute lamb's liver if you prefer.

SERVES 3–4

450g/1lb pig's or lamb's liver, trimmed and sliced
60ml/4 tbsp milk (for pig's liver)
30ml/2 tbsp olive oil
225g/8oz rindless smoked lean bacon rashers (strips), cut into pieces
2 onions, halved and sliced
175g/6oz/21/4 cups brown cap (cremini) mushrooms, halved
25g/1oz/2 tbsp butter
30ml/2 tbsp plain (all-purpose) flour
150ml/1/4 pint/2/3 cup hot chicken stock
15ml/1 tbsp soy sauce
5ml/1 tsp paprika
salt and ground black pepper

Directions

1 If using pig's liver, soak it in the milk for about 1 hour for a milder flavour, then blot the pig's liver dry with kitchen paper.

2 Heat the oil in a frying pan and stir-fry the bacon until crisp. Add the onion and cook, stirring, until softened. Add the mushrooms and fry for 1 minute.

3 Using a slotted spoon, remove the bacon and vegetables from the pan and keep warm. Add the liver to the fat remaining in the pan and cook over a high heat for 3–4 minutes, turning once to seal the slices on both sides. Remove from the pan and keep warm.

4 Melt the butter in the pan, sprinkle the flour over and cook briefly. Stir in thestock, soy sauce and paprika and bring to a simmer. Return the liver and vegetables. Simmer gently for 3–4 minutes. Check the seasoning.

Nutritional information per portion: Energy 386kcal/1610kJ; Protein 35.3g; Carbohydrate 8g, of which sugars 1.4g; Fat 23.9g, of which saturates 8.7g; Cholesterol 336mg; Calcium 29mg; Fibre 0.9g; Sodium 1267mg.

Fabada

This bean and sausage hotpot from the wild mountains of Asturias on the
northern coast of Spain, has achieved world fame. It used to contain dried broad beans, which gave it the name, but when modern fabes – white kidney beans – were adopted, it became a truly great dish.

SERVES 8

500–800g/11/4–13/4lb belly pork, in thick slices
1 smoked gammon (smoked or cured ham) knuckle, about 675g/11/2lb,
skin slashed
800g/13/4lb dried cannellini beans, soaked overnight
5ml/1 tsp black peppercorns, crushed
15ml/1 tbsp paprika
pinch of saffron threads (0.2g)
1 bay leaf
30ml/2 tbsp oil (optional)
4 garlic cloves, chopped
3 red chorizo sausages, thickly sliced
175g/6oz morcilla or black pudding (blood sausage), thickly sliced
ground black pepper (optional)

Directions

1 Put the pork belly and knuckle into a very large stockpot with water to cover. Bring to the boil, then drain the meat and return it to the stockpot.

2 Add the drained beans to the pot and pour over 2.3 litres/4 pints/10 cups water. Bring to the boil very slowly, then boil for 10 minutes. Reduce the heat and add the peppercorns, paprika, crumbled saffron and the bay leaf. Simmer very gently over a very low heat for 2 hours. Check occasionally that the beans are still covered with liquid, but stir carefully or the beans will break up.

3 Remove the pork belly and knuckle and set them aside to cool. Strip off the skin and fat, and take 30ml/ 2 tbsp chopped fat for frying (or use oil). Heat this in a frying pan and cook the garlic lightly, then spoon it into the beans. Fry the chorizo and morcilla or black pudding lightly in the pan. Gently stir into the bean pot.

4 Remove all the meat from the ham bone. Chop it with the pork and return to the stockpot. Simmer for a few minutes. Check the seasonings and serve.

COOK'S TIP

The quality of the bean is a feature of the dish so try to use luxury Spanish beans. Fabes are like very large, white cannellini beans. If luxury Spanish beans are unavailable use lingots (the French cassoulet bean).

Nutritional information per portion: Energy 741kcal/3106kJ; Protein 46.4g; Carbohydrate 59.6g, of which sugars 3.2g; Fat

36.9g, of which saturates 13.7g; Cholesterol 79mg; Calcium 106mg; Fibre 8.3g; Sodium 918mg.

Chorizo with Cooked Chestnuts

Native to Galicia, chestnuts are a popular addition to a variety of dishes.
Chorizos y castanas makes a good side dish for roast turkey and a popular
supper dish on its own. Add a little chilli for heat and spiciness.

SERVES 3–6

15ml/1 tbsp olive oil
4 red chorizo sausages, sliced
200g/7oz/11/4 cups peeled cooked chestnuts
15ml/1 tbsp paprika
salt and ground black pepper
crusty bread, to serve

Directions

1 Heat the oil in a wide frying pan and put in the chorizo slices in a single layer. Cook the chorizo for 3–4 minutes, turning frequently, until it starts to give off its oil.
2 Tip in the peeled chestnuts and toss until warm and covered with the chorizo oil. Add the paprika and season with the salt and ground black pepper. Serve hot with crusty bread.

Nutritional information per portion: Energy 180kcal/752kJ; Protein 4.2g; Carbohydrate 17g, of which sugars 2.9g; Fat 11.1g, of which saturates 3.8g; Cholesterol 13mg; Calcium 36mg; Fibre 1.5g; Sodium 275mg.

Albóndigas Con Salsa De Tomate

These tasty meatballs in tomato sauce are usually served in little brown,
individual casserole dishes, accompanied by crusty bread. They also make a good supper dish, with a green salad or pasta.

SERVES 4

225g/8oz minced (ground) beef
4 spring onions (scallions), thinly sliced
2 garlic cloves, finely chopped
30ml/2 tbsp grated fresh Parmesan cheese
10ml/2 tsp fresh thyme leaves
15ml/1 tbsp olive oil
3 tomatoes, chopped
30ml/2 tbsp red or dry white wine
10ml/2 tsp chopped fresh rosemary
pinch of sugar
salt and ground black pepper
fresh thyme, to garnish

Directions

1 Put the minced beef in a bowl. Add thc spring onions, garlic, Parmesan and thyme and of salt and pepper. Stir to mix, then shape the mixture into 12 small firm balls.

2 Heat the olive oil in a large, heavy frying pan and cook the meatballs for about 5 minutes, turning frequently, until evenly browned all over. Add the chopped tomatoes, wine, rosemary and sugar to the pan, with salt and ground black pepper to taste.
3 Cover the pan and cook gently for about 15 minutes until the meatballs are cooked through. Check the seasoning and serve, garnished with the thyme.

Nutritional information per portion: Energy 206kcal/856kJ; Protein 14.4g; Carbohydrate 5.2g, of whichsugars 5.1g; Fat 13.8g, of which saturates 5.5g; Cholesterol 38mg; Calcium 121mg; Fibre 1.5g; Sodium 133mg.

Black Bean Stew

Tolosa in the Basque country is famous for its black bean stew – potaje de alubiasnegras – made spicy with sausages and pickled pork. Here is a simplified version, with extra fresh vegetables.

SERVES 5–6

275g/10oz/11/2 cups black beans, soaked overnight in cold water
675g/11/2lb boneless belly pork rashers (strips)
60ml/4 tbsp olive oil
350g/12oz baby (pearl) onions
2 celery sticks, thickly sliced
150g/5oz chorizo, cut into chunks
10ml/2 tsp paprika
600ml/1 pint/21/2 cups light chicken or vegetable stock
2 green (bell) peppers, seeded and cut into large pieces
salt and ground black pepper

Directions

1 Drain the beans into a pan and cover with fresh water. Bring to the boil and boil rapidly for 10 minutes. Drain the beans and put in an ovenproof dish.
2 Preheat the oven to 160°C/325°F/Gas 3. Cut away any rind from the pork, then cut it into large chunks.

3 Heat the oil in a large frying pan and fry the onions and celery for 3 minutes. Add the pork and fry for 10 minutes, or until the pork is browned.

4 Add the chorizo and fry for 2 minutes, then sprinkle in the paprika. Tip the mixture into the beans and mix well to combine thoroughly.

5 Add the stock to the pan and bring to the boil, then pour over the meat and beans. Cover and bake for 1 hour.

6 Stir the green peppers into the stew and return to the oven for a further 15minutes. Season and serve hot.

Nutritional information per portion: Energy 760kcal/3159kJ; Protein 32.1g; Carbohydrate 37.3g, of which sugars 9.2g; Fat 54.7g, of which saturates 18.6g; Cholesterol 91mg; Calcium 85mg; Fibre 5.9g; Sodium 303mg.

Stuffed Roast Loin of Pork

Pork is Spain's most popular meat, particularly the loin. For this dish, lomo de cerdo relleno, you need the whole cut with the flap on the side to enclose the stuffing, which is flavoured with figs.

SERVES 4

60ml/4 tbsp olive oil
1 onion, finely chopped
2 garlic cloves, chopped
75g/3oz/11/2 cups stale breadcrumbs
4 ready-to-eat dried figs, chopped
8 pitted green olives, chopped
25g/1oz/1/4 cup flaked (sliced) almonds
15ml/1 tbsp lemon juice
15ml/1 tbsp chopped fresh parsley
1 egg yolk
1kg/21/4lb boned loin of pork with the side flap attached
salt, paprika and ground black pepper

Directions

1 Preheat the oven to 200°C/400°F/Gas 6. Heat 45ml/ 3 tbsp of the oil in a pan, add the onion and garlic, and cook gently until softened. Remove the pan from the heat, and stir in the breadcrumbs, figs, olives, almonds,

lemon juice, parsleyand egg yolk. Season with salt, paprika and pepper.

2 Remove any string from the pork and unroll the belly flap, cutting away any excess fat or meat to enable you to do so. Spread half the stuffing over the flat piece and roll it up, starting from the thick side. Tie the joint at intervals with string to hold it together.

3 Pour the remaining oil into a small roasting pan and add the pork. Roast for 11/4 hours. Meanwhile, form the remaining stuffing mixture into balls and add to the pan, 15–20 minutes before the end of cooking time.

4 Remove the pork from the oven and leave it to rest for 10 minutes. Carve into thick slices and serve with the stuffing balls and any juices from the pan. This dish is also good served cold.

Nutritional information per portion: Energy 732kcal/3065kJ; Protein 80.3g; Carbohydrate 25.6g, of which sugars 11.3g; Fat 34.9g, of which saturates 8.5g; Cholesterol 245mg; Calcium 133mg; Fibre 2.7g; Sodium 592mg.

Pork Empanada

This flat, two-crust Galician pie is famous because there is no occasion on which it is not served. It is festival food; it greets the boats of returning fishermen; and it is the men's lunchbox staple. Fillings vary enormously, and may include fish such as sardines, or scallops for special occasions.

SERVES 8

75ml/5 tbsp olive oil
2 onions, chopped
4 garlic cloves, finely chopped
1kg/21/4lb boned pork loin, diced
175g/6oz smoked gammon (smoked or cured ham) or raw ham, diced
3 red chorizo or other spicy sausages, about 300g/11oz
3 (bell) peppers mixed colours, seeded and chopped
175ml/6fl oz/3/2 cup white wine
200g/7oz can tomatoes
pinch of saffron threads (0.1g)
5ml/1 tsp paprika
30ml/2 tbsp chopped fresh parsley
salt and ground black pepper

FOR THE CORNMEAL DOUGH

250g/9oz cornmeal
7g/2 tsp easy-blend (rapid-rise) dried yeast
5ml/1 tsp caster (superfine) sugar
250g/9oz plain (all-purpose) flour, plus extra for dusting
5ml/1 tsp salt
200ml/7fl oz/scant 1 cup warm water
30ml/2 tbsp oil
2 eggs, beaten, plus 1 for the glaze

Directions

1 Make the filling. Heat 60ml/4 tbsp oil in a frying pan and fry the onions,
adding the garlic when the onions begin to colour. Transfer to a flameproof casserole. Add the pork and gammon or ham to the pan, and fry until coloured,stirring. Transfer to the casserole.
2 Add 15ml/1 tbsp oil, the sausage and the peppers to the pan and fry. Transfer to the casserole. Deglaze the pan with the wine, allowing it to bubble and reduce. Pour into the casserole.
3 Add the tomatoes, saffron, paprika and parsley and season. Cook gently for 20–30 minutes. Leave to cool.
4 Meanwhile make the dough. Put the cornmeal into a food processor. Add the dried yeast with the sugar. Gradually add the flour, salt, water, oil and two eggs and beat, to make a smooth soft dough.

5 Turn the dough into a clean bowl, cover with a dishtowel and leave in a warm place for 40–50 minutes, to rise.

6 Preheat the oven to 200°C/400°F/Gas 6. Grease a shallow roasting pan or dish 30 × 20cm/12 × 8in. Halve the dough. Roll out one half on a floured surface, a little larger than the pan. Lift this in place, leaving the border hanging over the edge.

7 Spoon in the filling. Roll out the lid and lay it in place. Fold the outside edge over the lid, trimming as necessary, and press gently all round with a fork to seal the pie. Prick the surface and brush with beaten egg.

8 Bake the pie for 30–35 minutes until golden, covering the ends if they brown too much. Cut the pie into squares.

Nutritional information per portion: Energy 704kcal/2944kJ; Protein 35.5g; Carbohydrate 58.6g, of which sugars 6.5g; Fat 35.6g, of which saturates 12.2g; Cholesterol 129mg; Calcium 97mg; Fibre 3.2g; Sodium 592mg.

Cocido

The Spanish national dish, cocido, is also Madrid's most famous stew. The name simply means "boiled dinner" and it used to be made more than once a week. The broth makes a soup course and then the rest is displayed on two splendid platters.

SERVES 8

500–800g/11/4–13/4lb cured brisket or silverside (pot roast)
250g/9oz smoked streaky (fatty) bacon, in one piece, or 250g/9oz belly pork
1 knuckle gammon (smoked or cured ham) bone, with some meat still attached
500–750g/11/4–13/4lb beef marrow bone, sawn through
1 pig's trotter (foot), sawn through
1 whole garlic bulb
2 bay leaves
5ml/1 tsp black peppercorns, lightly crushed

250g/9oz/11/4 cups dried chickpeas, soaked overnight and drained
2 quarters cornfed chicken
1 small onion, studded with 2 or 3 cloves
2 large carrots, cut into big pieces
2 leeks, cut into chunks
500g/11/4lb small new potatoes, scrubbed
2 red chorizo sausages
1 morcilla or 250g/9oz black pudding (blood sausage)
30ml/2 tbsp long grain rice
1 small (bell) pepper, finely diced
Salt

Directions

1 Put the salt meat – brisket or silverside, bacon or pork and knuckle – into alarge pan and cover with water. Bring slowly to the boil, simmer for 5 minutes to remove excess salt, and drain.
2 Using a very large stockpot (with a capacity of at least 6 litres/10 pints/5 quarts), pack in all the meat, skinside down, with the marrowbone and trotter. Add the garlic bulb, bay leaves and peppercorns, with water to cover. Bring to simmering point, skimming off any scum, with a slotted spoon.
3 Add the drained chickpeas, cover and simmer on the lowest possible heat for 11/2 hours, checking occasionally that there is enough liquid. Add the chicken and onion to the pot. Cook until the chickpeas are done.

4 Start the vegetables. Put the carrots, leeks and potatoes into a large pan with the chorizo (but not the morcilla or black pudding). Cover with water and bring to the boil. Simmer for 25 minutes, until the potatoes are cooked. About 5 minutes before the end, add the morcilla or black pudding.

5 Strain off enough broth from the meat pot (about 1.2 litres/2 pints/5 cups) into a pan, for soup. Bring back to the boil, sprinkle in the rice and cook for 15 minutes. Add the diced pepper and cook for 2–3 minutes more. Serve the soup as the first course.

6 Drain the vegetables and sausages and arrange on a platter. Serve as a separate second course or as an accompaniment with the meat.

7 Slice the meats, removing the marrow from the bone and adding it to the chickpeas. Arrange with all the meats on a heated serving platter, moistening with a little broth.

Nutritional information per portion: Energy 593kcal/2478kJ; Protein 46.4g; Carbohydrate 37g, of which sugars 4.5g; Fat 29.6g, of which saturates 10.1g; Cholesterol 138mg; Calcium 116mg; Fibre 5.3g; Sodium 1100mg.

Lamb with Red Peppers and Rioja

World-famous for its red wine, Rioja also produces excellent red peppers. It even has a red pepper fair, at Lodoso, every year. Together they give this lamb stew a lovely rich flavour. Boiled potatoes make a very good accompaniment.

SERVES 4

15ml/1 tbsp plain (all-purpose) flour
1kg/21/4lb lean lamb, cubed
60ml/4 tbsp olive oil
2 red onions, sliced
4 garlic cloves, sliced
10ml/2 tsp paprika
1.5ml/1/4 tsp ground cloves
400ml/14fl oz/12/3 cups red Rioja
150ml/1/4 pint/2/3 cup lamb stock
2 bay leaves
2 thyme sprigs
3 red (bell) peppers, halved and seeded
salt and ground black pepper
bay leaves and thyme sprigs, to garnish (optional)

Directions

1 Preheat the oven to 160°C/325°F/Gas 3. Season the flour, add the lamb and toss lightly to coat.

2 Heat the oil in a pan and fry the lamb until browned. Transfer to an ovenproof dish. Fry the onions and garlic until soft. Add to the meat.

3 Add the paprika, cloves, Rioja, lamb stock, bay leaves and thyme and then bring the mixture to a gentle simmer.

4 Add the halved and seeded red peppers. Cover the dish with a lid or foil and cook for about 30 minutes, or until the meat is tender.

5 Check the seasoning. Garnish with more bay leaves and thyme sprigs, if you like.

Nutritional information per portion: Energy 635kcal/2646kJ; Protein 49.8g; Carbohydrate 4.1g, of which sugars 0.4g; Fat 39.4g, of which saturates 14.6g; Cholesterol 190mg; Calcium 37mg; Fibre 0.2g; Sodium 223mg.

Veal Casserole with Broad Beans

This delicate stew, flavoured with sherry and plenty of garlic, is a spring dish made with new vegetables – menestra de ternera. For a delicious flavour be sure to add plenty of parsley just before serving. Lamb is equally good cooked in this way.

SERVES 6

45ml/3 tbsp olive oil
1.3–1.6kg/3–31/2lb veal, cut into 5cm/2in cubes
1 large onion, chopped
6 large garlic cloves, unpeeled
1 bay leaf
5ml/1 tsp paprika
240ml/8fl oz/1 cup fino sherry
100g/4oz/scant 1 cup shelled, skinned broad (fava) beans
60ml/4 tbsp chopped fresh flat leaf parsley
salt and ground black pepper

Directions

1 Heat 30ml/2 tbsp oil in a large, heavy pan. Add half the meat and brown well on all sides. Transfer to a plate. Brown the rest of the meat and remove from the pan.

2 Add the remaining oil to the pan and cook the onion until soft. Return the meat and stir well to mix with the onion.
3 Add the garlic cloves, bay leaf, paprika and sherry. Season with salt and black pepper. Cover and cook very gently for 30–40 minutes.
4 Add the broad beans to the pan about 10 minutes before the end of the cooking time. Check the seasoning and stir in the chopped parsley just before serving.

Nutritional information per portion: Energy 352kcal/1473kJ; Protein 47.4g; Carbohydrate 3.6g, of whichsugars 1.3g; Fat 11.6g, of which saturates 2.8g; Cholesterol 182mg; Calcium 34mg; Fibre 1.2g; Sodium 244mg.

Lamb Cochifrito

Aragon and Navarre in the Pyrenees are known for their fine ingredients – and also for their simple cooking.

SERVES 4

800g/13/4lb very well-trimmed, tender lamb, in cubes or strips
30ml/2 tbsp olive oil, plus extra
1 onion, chopped
2 garlic cloves, finely chopped
5ml/1 tsp paprika
juice of 2 lemons
15ml/1 tbsp finely chopped fresh parsley
salt and ground black pepper

Directions

1 Season the lamb with salt and ground black pepper. Heat the 30ml/2 tbsp olive oil in a large frying pan over a high heat and add the meat in handfuls. Add the onion at the same time, and keep pushing the meat around the pan. Add more meat to the pan as each batch is sealed. Add the chopped garlic and a little more oil if necessary.

2 When the meat is golden and the onion soft, sprinkle with paprika and lemon juice. Cover and simmer for 15

minutes. Check the seasonings and sprinkle with the parsley, then serve.

Nutritional information per portion: Energy 424kcal/1766kJ; Protein 40.1g; Carbohydrate 2.3g, of which sugars 1.1g; Fat 28.4g, of which saturates 11.2g; Cholesterol 152mg; Calcium 44mg; Fibre 0.7g; Sodium 177mg.

Skewered Lamb with Red Onion Salsa

The Moors first introduced skewered and barbecued meat to Spain, where it has been popular for over 1,500 years.

SERVES 4

500–675g/11/4–11/2lb ready-trimmed, cubed lamb
5ml/1 tsp ground cumin
10ml/2 tsp paprika
30ml/2 tbsp olive oil
salt and ground black pepper

FOR THE RED ONION SALSA
1 red onion, very thinly sliced
1 large tomato, seeded and chopped
15ml/1 tbsp red wine vinegar
3–4 fresh basil or mint leaves, roughly torn

Directions

1 Season the lamb with the cumin, paprika, oil and black pepper. Toss well to coat. Leave in a refrigerator overnight. Then, spear the cubes of lamb on four skewers, leaving one end of each of the skewers free for picking up.
2 To make the salsa, put the onion, tomato, vinegar and basil or mint in a small bowl and mix. Season to taste.

3 Cook on a barbecue or preheat the grill (broiler) with the shelf about 15cm/6in from the heat. Generously brush the grill pan with oil.

4 Season the lamb with salt and cook for 5–10 minutes, turning the skewers, until the lamb is well browned but still slightly pink in the centre. Serve hot, with the salsa.

Nutritional information per portion: Energy 294kcal/1224kJ; Protein 25.4g; Carbohydrate 3.3g, of which sugars 1.6g; Fat 20.1g, of which saturates 7.4g; Cholesterol 95mg; Calcium 22mg; Fibre 0.5g; Sodium 112mg.

Solomillo with Cabrales Sauce

Well-hung beef is a feature of the Basque country, served here with Cabrales, the blue cheese from Spain's northern mountains. French Roquefort is also extremely popular.

SERVES 4

25g/1oz/2 tbsp butter
30ml/2 tbsp olive oil
4 fillet steaks, cut 5cm/2in thick, about 150g/5oz each
salt and coarsely ground black pepper
fresh flat leaf parsley, to garnish

FOR THE BLUE CHEESE SAUCE
30ml/2 tbsp Spanish brandy
150ml/5fl oz/2/3 cup double (heavy) cream
75g/3oz Cabrales or Roquefort cheese, crumbled

Directions

1 Heat the butter and oil together in a heavy frying pan, over a high heat. Season the steaks well. Fry them for 2 minutes on each side, to sear them.

2 Lower the heat slightly and cook for a further 2–3 minutes on each side, or according to your taste. Remove the steaks to a warm plate.

3 To make the sauce, reduce the heat and add the brandy, stirring to pick up the juices. Add the cream and boil to reduce a little.

4 Add the crumbled cheese and mash it into the sauce using a spoon. Taste for seasoning. Serve in a small sauce jug (pitcher), or poured over the steaks. Garnish the beef with parsley.

Nutritional information per portion: Energy 573kcal/2374kJ; Protein 36.3g; Carbohydrate 0.7g, of which sugars 0.7g; Fat 45.4g, of which saturates 24.4g; Cholesterol 170mg; Calcium 117mg; Fibre 0g; Sodium 341mg.

Rabo De Toro

In the Spanish kitchen, the most famous part of the bull is his tail – although most people are more likely to cook with oxtail. This stew can be prepared several days ahead.

SERVES 6

60ml/4 tbsp olive oil
2 onions, chopped
1.6kg/31/2lb oxtail, chopped across
30ml/2 tbsp plain (all-purpose) flour, seasoned with salt, paprika and
pepper
6 carrots, cut into short lengths
2 large garlic cloves, smashed
1 bay leaf
2 thyme sprigs
2 leeks, thinly sliced
1 clove
pinch of freshly grated nutmeg
350ml/12fl oz/11/2 cups red wine
30ml/2 tbsp vinegar
350ml/12fl oz/11/2 cups stock
30ml/2 tbsp fino sherry
60ml/4 tbsp chopped fresh parsley
salt, paprika and black pepper
boiled potatoes, to serve

Directions

1 Preheat the oven to 150°C/300°F/Gas 2. Heat 30ml/ 2 tbsp oil in a large frying pan, add the onions and fry until softened. Remove to a casserole.

2 Dust the oxtail pieces all over with the seasoned flour. Add the remaining oil tothe pan and put in the oxtail pieces. Fry, turning them to brown all over, thenfit into the casserole, standing upright in a single layer.

3 Push the carrots into the spaces between the pieces of oxtail. Tuck in the garlic cloves, bay leaf and thyme sprigs and add the leeks. Add the clove, grated nutmeg and more black pepper. Pour in the wine, vinegar and enough stock to cover. Bring to simmering point, then cover the casserole with a lid. Cook in the oven for about 3 hours, or until the meat is falling off the bones.

4 Skim the fat off the top of the stew. Spoon the larger meat pieces on to a plate and remove the bones and fat. Push all the remaining oxtail and carrots to one end of the pan and discard the bay leaf and thyme. Spoon the garlic and some of the soft vegetables into a food processor and purée with the sherry. Return the meat and purée to the casserole and heat through. Stir in the parsley, check the seasonings and serve with boiled potatoes.

Nutritional information per portion: Energy 392kcal/1638kJ; Protein 32.1g; Carbohydrate 8.1g, of which sugars 4g; Fat 21.1g, of which saturates 1.1g; Cholesterol 0mg; Calcium 39mg; Fibre 1g; Sodium 199mg.

RopaVieja

The name of this dish means "old clothes", which sounds much more romantic than leftovers. It is a dish for using up meats from the cocido, and the recipe shows both Jewish and Arab influences.

SERVES 4

2 small aubergines (eggplants), cubed
90ml/6 tbsp olive oil
1 large onion, chopped
3 garlic cloves, finely chopped
1 fresh, or baked, red (bell) pepper, seeded and sliced (optional)
400g/14oz can tomatoes
250ml/8fl oz/1 cup meat stock
2.5ml/1/2 tsp ground allspice
2.5ml/1/2 tsp ground cumin pinch of ground cloves
2.5ml/1/2 tsp cayenne pepper
400g/14oz cooked beef, cubed, or mixed turkey, ham, etc
400g/14oz can chickpeas, drained
salt and ground black pepper
chopped fresh mint, to garnish (optional)

Directions

1 Put the aubergine cubes into a colander. Sprinkle with 10ml/2 tsp salt, turning the cubes over. Leave to drain for 1 hour. Rinse, then squeeze them dry using kitchen paper.

2 Meanwhile put 30ml/2 tbsp oil in a large, heavy pan and fry the onion and garlic until soft. If using a fresh pepper, add it to the pan and stir-fry until softened.

3 Add the tomatoes, stock, allspice, cumin, cloves, cayenne and the baked

pepper, if using. Season to taste. Add the meat and simmer.

4 Heat 45ml/3 tbsp oil over a high heat in a frying pan. Fry the aubergine cubesuntil they are brown on all sides.

5 Add the aubergine and chickpeas to the large pan and bring to a simmer, adding a little more stock to cover – the dish should be almost solid. Check the seasonings, garnish with mint, if using, and serve.

Nutritional information per portion: Energy 486kcal/2029kJ; Protein 31.9g; Carbohydrate 24.8g, of which sugars 8.5g; Fat 29.5g, of which saturates 6.7g; Cholesterol 58mg; Calcium 70mg; Fibre 7.5g; Sodium 297mg.

Rabbit Salmorejo

The Carthaginians and Romans named Spain "Rabbit Land". The modernname, España, is derived from the Latin Hispania and reminds us howcommon rabbits, and rabbit dishes, are in Spain.

SERVES 4

675g/11/2lb rabbit, jointed
300ml/1/2 pint/11/4 cups dry white wine
15ml/1 tbsp sherry vinegar
several oregano sprigs
2 bay leaves
30ml/2 tbsp plain (all-purpose) flour
90ml/6 tbsp olive oil
175g/6oz baby (pearl) onions, peeled and left whole
4 garlic cloves, sliced
150ml/1/4 pint/2/3 cup chicken stock
1 dried chilli, seeded and finely chopped
10ml/2 tsp paprika
salt and ground black pepper
fresh flat leaf parsley sprigs, to garnish (optional)

Directions

1 Put the rabbit in a bowl. Add the wine, vinegar, oregano and bay leaves and toss together. Marinate for several hours or overnight in the refrigerator.

2 Drain the rabbit, reserving the marinade, and pat it dry with kitchen paper. Season the flour and use to dust the marinated rabbit.

3 Heat the oil in a large, wide flameproof casserole or frying pan. Fry the rabbit pieces until golden on all sides, then remove them and set aside. Fry the onions until they are beginning to colour, then reserve on a separate plate.

4 Add the garlic to the pan and fry, then add the strained marinade, with the chicken stock, chilli and paprika.

5 Return the rabbit and the reserved onions to the pan. Bring to a simmer, then cover and simmer gently for about 45 minutes until the rabbit is tender. Check the seasoning, adding more vinegar and paprika if necessary. Serve the dish garnished with a few sprigs of flat leaf parsley, if you like.

Nutritional information per portion: Energy 311kcal/1294kJ; Protein 23.2g; Carbohydrate 9.5g, of which sugars 2.6g; Fat 20.4g, of which saturates 4.1g; Cholesterol 83mg; Calcium 65mg; Fibre 0.9g; Sodium52mg.

Carne Con Chocolate

Chocolatecame to Europe via Spain. It is not naturally sweet and so chocolate squares are used in Spain in the way that other countries use gravy browning. It gives this stew a rich darkness.

SERVES 6

60ml/4 tbsp olive oil
1kg/21/4lb trimmed stewing beef
5ml/1 tsp paprika
150g/5oz smoked bacon lardons, or pancetta
1 large Spanish (Bermuda) onion, chopped
4 carrots, thickly sliced
1 large leek, white only, sliced
6 garlic cloves, crushed
225g/8oz brown cap (cremini) mushrooms, sliced
4 tomatoes, peeled, seeded and chopped
45ml/3 tbsp plain (all-purpose) flour
12 peppercorns, crushed
1 pig's trotter (foot), sawn through
250ml/8fl oz/1 cup dry red wine
1 bay leaf
4 sprigs of thyme
120ml/4fl oz/1/2 cup Spanish brandy
300ml/10fl oz/11/4 cups meat stock
450g/1lb small potatoes, peeled
25g/1oz dark (bittersweet) chocolate, grated

salt and ground black pepper
45ml/3 tbsp chopped fresh parsley, to garnish

Directions

1 Preheat the oven to 180°C/350°F/Gas 4. Heat 30ml/2 tbsp oil in a frying pan.Season the beef with paprika and fry in two batches, over a high heat, turning until browned on all sides. Reserve the first batch on a plate when done. Add a little more oil and fry the second batch.

2 Meanwhile heat 15ml/1 tbsp oil in a large flameproof casserole and fry the bacon or pancetta. When the fat starts to run, add the onion, carrots and leek and cook gently until the onion softens.

3 Add the garlic to the pan, together with the mushrooms and tomatoes. Stir and cook gently, then sprinkle with the flour and cook briefly.

4 Add the meat, peppercorns and salt to the casserole. Tuck in the trotter. Add a little wine, stir to deglaze, then add all the wine, stirring. Add the bay leaf and thyme. Pour in brandy and stock to cover. Return to a simmer, then cover and cook in the oven for 11/4 hours.

5 Cook the potatoes in a pan of boiling water for 15 minutes. Add them to the casserole with the chocolate. Simmer for 30 minutes. Remove the trotter and serve, sprinkled with parsley.

Nutritional information per portion: Energy 648kcal/2705kJ; Protein 46.1g; Carbohydrate 29.8g, of which sugars 12.1g; Fat 31g, of which saturates 10.4g; Cholesterol 113mg; Calcium 62mg; Fibre 4.6g; Sodium459mg.

Venison Chops with Romesco Sauce

Romesco is the Catalan word for the ñora chilli. It lends a spicy roundness to one of Spain's greatest sauces. It can be served cold as a dip, but this version is the ideal partner for game chops.

SERVES 4

4 venison chops, cut 2cm/3/4in thick and about 175–200g/6–7oz each
30ml/2 tbsp olive oil
50g/2oz/4 tbsp butter
braised Savoy cabbage, to serve

FOR THE SAUCE
3 ñora chillies
1 hot dried chilli
25g/1oz/1/4 cup almonds
150ml/1/4 pint/2/3 cup olive oil
1 slice stale bread, crusts removed
3 garlic cloves, chopped
3 tomatoes, peeled, seeded and roughly chopped
60ml/4 tbsp sherry vinegar
60ml/4 tbsp red wine vinegar
salt and ground black pepper

Directions

1 To make the romesco sauce, slit the chillies and remove the seeds, then leave the chillies to soak in warm water for 30 minutes until soft. Drain the chillies, dry them on kitchen paper and chop finely.

2 Dry-fry the almonds in a frying pan over a medium heat, shaking the pan occasionally, until the nuts are toasted evenly. Transfer the nuts to a food processor or blender.

3 Add 45ml/3 tbsp oil to the pan and fry the bread slice until golden on bothsides. Lift it out with a slotted spoon and drain on kitchen paper. Tear the bread and add to the food processor or blender. Fry the garlic in the remaining oil.

4 Add the soaked chillies and tomatoes to the processor or blender. Tip in the garlic, with the oil from the pan and blend the mixture to form a smooth paste. With the motor running, gradually add the remaining olive oil and then the sherry and wine vinegars. When the sauce is smooth, scrape it into a bowl and season to taste. Cover with clear film (plastic wrap) and chill for 2 hours.

5 Season the chops with pepper. Heat the olive oil and butter in a heavy frying pan and fry the chops for about 5 minutes each side until golden brown and cooked through. When the chops are almost cooked, transfer the sauce to a pan and heat it gently. If it is too thick, stir in a little boiling water. Serve the sauce with the chops, accompanied by braised cabbage.

Nutritional information per portion: Energy 415kcal/1741kJ; Protein 46.9g; Carbohydrate 6.2g, of which sugars 2.9g; Fat 24g, of which saturates 9.3g; Cholesterol 127mg; Calcium 40mg; Fibre 1.3g; Sodium229mg.

Desserts and Baking

Iced desserts were introduced to Spain by the Moors, who also created luxurious dishes of fruit in syrups. Caramel is a much-loved flavour and is used in a winter fruit salad of oranges and a "drunken" cake soaked in brandy. As well as desserts this chapter has delicious pastries and cookies, breakfast rolls and satisfying, solid loaves.

Honey-Baked Figs with Hazelnut Ice Cream

Two wild ingredients – figs and hazelnuts – are used to make this delectable dessert, higos con helado de avellana. Fresh figs are baked in a lightly spiced lemon and honey syrup and are served with home-made roasted hazelnut ice cream.

SERVES 4

finely pared rind of 1 lemon
1 cinnamon stick, roughly broken
60ml/4 tbsp clear honey
8 large figs

FOR THE HAZELNUT ICE CREAM
450ml/3/4 pint/scant 2 cups double (heavy) cream

50g/2oz/1/4 cup caster (superfine) sugar
3 large (US extra large) egg yolks
1.5ml/1/4 tsp vanilla extract
75g/3oz/3/4 cup hazelnuts

Directions

1 Make the ice cream. Gently heat the cream in a pan until almost boiling.
Meanwhile, beat the sugar and egg yolks in a bowl until creamy.
2 Pour a little hot cream into the egg yolk mixture and stir with a wooden spoon. Pour back into the pan and mix well. Cook over a low heat, stirring constantly, until the mixture thickens slightly and lightly coats the back of the spoon – do not allow it to boil.
3 Pour the custard into a bowl, stir in the vanilla extract and leave to cool.
4 Preheat the oven to 180°C/350°F/Gas 4. Place the hazelnuts on a baking sheet and roast for 10–12 minutes, or until golden. Leave the nuts to cool, then grind them in a food processor.
5 If you have an ice cream machine, pour in the cold custard and churn until halfset. Add the ground hazelnuts and continue to churn until the ice cream is thick. Freeze until firm.
6 Working by hand, pour the custard into a freezerproof container and freeze for 2 hours, or until the custard feels firm around the edges. Turn into a bowl and beat with an electric whisk or turn into a food

processor and beat until smooth. Stir in the hazelnuts and freeze until half set. Beat once more, then freeze until firm.

7 Preheat the oven to 200°C/400°F/Gas 6. Remove the ice cream from the freezer and allow to soften slightly.

8 To make the syrup, put the lemon rind, cinnamon stick, honey and 200ml/7fl oz/scant 1 cup water in a small pan and heat slowly until boiling. Simmer the mixture for 5 minutes, then leave to stand for 15 minutes.

9 Using a sharp knife, cut the figs almost into quarters but leaving the figs still attached at the base. Pack them into a casserole, in a single layer, and pour the honey syrup round and over them. Cover the dish tightly with foil and bake for 10 minutes.

10 Arrange the figs on small serving plates, with the cooking syrup poured round them. Serve accompanied by a scoop or two of the ice cream.

Nutritional information per portion: Energy 917kcal/3805kJ; Protein 8.3g; Carbohydrate 50.5g, of which sugars 50.1g; Fat 77.2g, of which saturates 39.7g; Cholesterol 311mg; Calcium 207mg; Fibre 4.2g; Sodium 60mg.

Rum and Raisin Ice Cream

Helado con ron y pasas is an ice cream with a long tradition in Spain. Dark rum comes from the former Spanish island of Cuba, while the Malaga region produces huge, black Muscatel raisins.

SERVES 4–6

150g/5oz/1 cup large Muscatel raisins, Malagan if possible
60ml/4 tbsp dark rum
4 egg yolks
75g/3oz/6 tbsp light brown sugar
5ml/1 tsp cornflour (cornstarch)
300ml/1/2 pint/11/4 cups full-fat (whole) milk
300ml/1/2 pint/11/4 cups whipping cream
wafers or biscuits (cookies), to serve

Directions

1 Put the raisins in a bowl, add the rum and mix well. Cover and leave to soak for 3–4 hours or overnight.
2 Whisk together the egg yolks, sugar and cornflour in a bowl until thick and foamy. Heat the milk in a pan to just below boiling point.
3 Whisk the milk into the eggs, then pour back into the pan. Cook over a gentle heat, stirring with a wooden

spoon, until the custard thickens and is smooth. Leave to cool.

4 Whip the cream until it is just thick, then fold it into the custard. Working by hand, pour the mixture into a freezerproof container. Freeze for 4 hours, beating once in a food processor after 2 hours, then beat again after 4 hours.

5 Fold the soaked raisins into the ice cream, then cover and freeze for 2–3 hours, or until it is firm enough to scoop. Serve the ice cream in bowls or tall glasses, with wafers or dessert biscuits.

Nutritional information per portion: Energy 397kcal/1654kJ; Protein 5.2g; Carbohydrate 34.9g, of whichsugars 34.1g; Fat 24.8g, of which saturates 14.2g; Cholesterol 190mg; Calcium 123mg; Fibre 0.5g; Sodium 56mg.

Sorbete De Limón

The Moors introduced ices to Andalucia a thousand years ago. Eating this smooth, tangy sorbet, you can imagine yourself in a palace like the one at Granada, lounging on silken cushions.

SERVES 6

200g/7oz/1 cup caster (superfine) sugar
300ml/1/4 pint/11/4 cups water
4 lemons, washed
1 large (US extra large) egg white
a little sugar, for sprinkling

Directions

1 Put the sugar and water into a heavy pan and bring slowly to the boil, stirring occasionally, until the sugar has just dissolved.

2 Pare the rind from two of the lemons directly into the pan. Simmer for 2 minutes without stirring, then remove from the heat. Leave the syrup to cool, then chill.

3 Squeeze the juice from all the lemons and strain it into the syrup, making sure all the pips (seeds) are removed. Take the rind out of the syrup and set it aside for the garnish.

4 Working by hand, strain the syrup into a plastic tub or a similar shallow
Freezerproof container and freeze for 4 hours, until the mixture is mushy.

5 Scoop the mixture into a food processor and beat until smooth. Whisk the egg white with a fork until it is just frothy. Spoon the sorbet back into its container and beat in the egg white. Freeze for 1 hour.

6 To make the garnish, cut the rind into strips and sprinkle with sugar. Scoop the sorbet into bowls and decorate with sugared lemon rind.

Nutritional information per portion: Energy 135kcal/574kJ; Protein 0.7g; Carbohydrate 35.1g, of whichsugars 35.1g; Fat 0g, of which saturates 0g; Cholesterol 0mg; Calcium 19mg; Fibre 0g; Sodium 12mg.

Bitter Chocolate Mousses

The Spanish introduced chocolate to Europe, and chocolate mousse remains a favourite dessert. These lovely cremas de chocolate are rich with chocolate, with a hint of orange from the liqueur.

SERVES 8

225g/8oz dark (bittersweet) chocolate, chopped
30ml/2 tbsp orange liqueur or a good Spanish brandy such as Torres
50g/2oz/1/4 cup unsalted (sweet) butter, cut into small pieces
4 large (US extra large) eggs, separated
90ml/6 tbsp whipping cream
45ml/3 tbsp caster (superfine) sugar

Directions

1 Place the chocolate and 60ml/4 tbsp water in a pan. Melt over a low heat, stirring. Off the heat whisk in the liqueur or brandy and butter. Beat the egg yolks until thick and creamy, then slowly beat into the chocolate until blended.

2 Whip the cream until soft peaks form, then stir a spoonful into the chocolate mixture to lighten it. Gently fold in the remaining whipped cream.

3 In a clean, grease-free bowl, use an electric mixer to slowly whisk the egg whites until frothy. Increase the

speed and continue until the egg whites form soft peaks. Gradually sprinkle the sugar over the egg whites and continue beating until the whites are stiff and glossy.

4 Stir a quarter of the egg whites into the chocolate mixture to lighten it, then gently fold in the remaining whites, cutting down to the bottom of the bowl, along the sides and up to the top in a semi-circular motion until they are just combined. Gently spoon the mixture into eight individual dishes or a 2 litre/31/2 pint/8 cup bowl. Chill for at least 2 hours until set before serving.

Nutritional information per portion: Energy 300kcal/1251kJ; Protein 4.8g; Carbohydrate 24.1g, of which sugars 23.8g; Fat 20.3g, of which saturates 11.6g; Cholesterol 122mg; Calcium 34mg; Fibre 0.7g; Sodium

Crema Catalana

This fabulous dessert of creamy custard topped with a net of brittle sugar may be the origin of all crème brûlées. Cremat is the Catalan word for “burnt”, and was probably part of the original name.

SERVES 4

475ml/16fl oz/2 cups milk
pared rind of 1/2 lemon
1 cinnamon stick
4 large (US extra large) egg yolks
105ml/7 tbsp caster (superfine) sugar
25ml/11/2 tbsp cornflour (cornstarch)
ground nutmeg, for sprinkling

Directions

1 Put the milk in a pan with the lemon rind and cinnamon stick. Bring to the boil, then simmer for 10 minutes. Remove the lemon rind and cinnamon. Put the egg yolks and 45ml/3 tbsp sugar in a bowl, and whisk until pale yellow. Add the cornflour and mix well.

2 Stir a few tablespoons of the hot milk into the egg yolk mixture, then tip back into the remaining milk. Return to the heat and cook gently, stirring, for about 5 minutes, until thickened and smooth. Do not boil.

3 Pour the custard into four shallow ovenproof dishes, about 13cm/5in in
diameter. Once cool, chill for a few hours, or overnight, until firm.
4 No more than 30 minutes before serving, sprinkle each dessert with 15ml/1 tbsp of the sugar and a little nutmeg. Preheat the grill (broiler) to high. Place the dishes under the grill, on the highest shelf, and cook for a few seconds until the sugar has caramelized. Remove the custards and leave to cool for a few minutes before serving.

Nutritional information per portion: Energy 244kcal/1030kJ; Protein 7.2g; Carbohydrate 38.8g, of whichsugars 33g; Fat 7.8g, of which saturates 2.9g; Cholesterol 217mg; Calcium 182mg; Fibre 0g; Sodium 65mg.

Arrope

This is an old Arab recipe whose name means "syrup"; this version comes from the Pyrenees. Arrope starts as a lovely fruit compote and ends up as a syrupy jam, to be scooped up with bread.

SERVES 10

3 firm peaches, unpeeled
1kg/21/4lb/5 cups sugar
3 large eating apples
finely grated rind of 1 lemon
3 firm pears
finely grated rind of 1 orange
1 small sweet potato, 150g/5oz prepared weight
200g/7oz butternut squash, peeled and prepared weight
250ml/8fl oz/1 cup dark rum
30ml/2 tbsp clear honey

Directions

1 Cut the peaches into eighths, without peeling them, and place in the bottom of a large, heavy pan. Sprinkle with 15ml/1 tbsp of the sugar. Peel and core the apples and cut them into 16 segments, then arrange on top of the peaches. Sprinkle the lemon rind over the top, along with 15ml/1 tbsp of the sugar. Prepare the pears

in the same way as the apples, place in the pan, then sprinkle over the orange rind, followed by 15ml/1 tbsp of the sugar.

2 Slice the sweet potato into pieces half the size of the pears and spread them over the top. Prepare the squash in the same way, layering it on top. Sprinkle about 15ml/1 tbsp of the sugar. Cover with a plate that fits inside the rim, and weigh down with a couple of cans. Stand for a minimum of 2 to 12 hours for juice to form.

3 Remove the cans and plate, put the pan over a fairly low heat and bring to asimmer. Cook and soften the fruit for 20 minutes, stirring once or twice to prevent sticking.

4 Add the remaining sugar, in batches, stirring to dissolve each batch before adding the next. Bring the mixture up to a rolling boil, over a medium high heat, and boil very steadily for 45 minutes. Stir and lift off any scum. The syrup should be considerably reduced. Test by pouring a spoonful on a plate. It should wrinkle when a spoon is pulled across.

5 Off the heat, add the rum and honey and stir well to combine. Return the pan to a moderate heat and cook for a further 10 minutes, stirring to prevent the fruit sticking. Remove the pan from the heat and set aside to cool. If the resulting compote is too stiff, stir in some more rum before serving.

Nutritional information per portion: Energy 516kcal/2194kJ; Protein 1.4g; Carbohydrate 120.8g, of which sugars 118.3g; Fat 0.2g, of which saturates 0g; Cholesterol 0mg; Calcium 71mg; Fibre 2.6g; Sodium 15mg.

Hazelnut Meringues with Nectarines

Meringues go back to Moorish times and hazelnuts are a popular flavouring. Here they are served with cream whipped with Malaga's dessert wine, and stuffed with fresh nectarines.

SERVES 5

3 large (US extra large) egg whites
175g/6oz/generous 3/4 cup caster (superfine) sugar
50g/2oz/1/2 cup chopped hazelnuts, toasted
300ml/1/2 pint/11/4 cups double (heavy) Cream
60ml/4 tbsp sweet Malaga dessert wine
2 nectarines, stoned (pitted) and sliced
fresh mint sprigs, to decorate

Directions

1 Preheat the oven to 140°C/275°F/Gas 1. Line two large baking sheets with baking parchment.
2 Whisk the egg whites in a grease-free bowl until they form stiff peaks.
Gradually whisk in the sugar a spoonful at a time, until a stiff, glossy meringue forms. Fold two-thirds of the hazelnuts into the egg whites.
3 Divide the meringue mixture between the baking sheets, spooning five ovals on to each one. Sprinkle the remaining hazelnuts over the meringues on one baking

sheet, then flatten the tops of the others using the back of a spoon.

4 Bake the meringues for 1–11/4 hours until crisp and dry, then lift them off the baking parchment and leave to cool.

5 Put the cream and dessert wine in a bowl and whisk to form soft peaks. Spoon a little of the cream on to each of the plain meringues. Arrange a few nectarine slices on each. Put one cream-topped meringue and one nut-topped meringue on each plate. Garnish with fresh mint and serve immediately.

Nutritional information per portion: Energy 539kcal/2247kJ; Protein 5g; Carbohydrate 43.6g, of which sugars 43.4g; Fat 38.6g, of which saturates 20.5g; Cholesterol 82mg; Calcium 68mg; Fibre 1.3g; Sodium 54mg.

Oranges with Caramel Wigs

Naranjas con pelucas is a pretty variation on the normal orange salad. The caramelized rind and syrup has a wonderful flavour that contrasts with the oranges.

SERVES 6

6 oranges
120g/4oz/generous 1/2 cup caster (superfine) sugar
120ml/4fl oz/1/2 cup boiling water
cocktail sticks (toothpicks)

Directions

1 Thinly pare 12 long strips of orange rind. Peel all the oranges, reserving the rind and discarding the pith. Reserve the juice and freeze the oranges separately for 30 minutes.
2 Slice the oranges horizontally, reform and secure with a cocktail stick. Chill.
3 To make the wigs, simmer the rind for about 5 minutes, drain, rinse, and then repeat. Trim with scissors.
4 Put half the sugar into a pan with 15ml/1 tbsp water. Heat gently until the mixture caramelizes. When it colours, dip the pan into cold water. Add 30ml/2 tbsp hot water and the rind. Stir until the caramel dissolves. Cool the rind.

5 Make a caramel syrup for serving as before. When it has coloured, stand back, pour in the boiling water and stir with a wooden spoon to dissolve. Add the reserved juices and pour into a jug (pitcher).

6 To serve, arrange the orange strips on top of each orange. Remove the cocktail sticks and pour a little caramel syrup round each orange.

Nutritional information per portion: Energy 122kcal/521kJ; Protein 1.4g; Carbohydrate 30.8g, of which sugars 30.8g; Fat 0.1g, of which saturates 0g; Cholesterol 0mg; Calcium 66mg; Fibre 2g; Sodium 7mg.

Leche Frita with Black Fruit Sauce

The name of this dessert means "fried milk", but it is really custard squares. It is very popular in the Basque country, and has a melting, creamy centre and crunchy, golden coating.

SERVES 6–8

550ml/18fl oz/21/2 cups full-fat (whole) milk
3 finely pared strips of lemon rind
1/2 cinnamon stick
90g/31/2oz/1/2 cup caster (superfine) sugar, plus extra for sprinkling
60ml/4 tbsp cornflour (cornstarch)
30ml/2 tbsp plain (all-purpose) flour
3 large (US extra large) egg yolks
2 large (US extra large) eggs
90–120ml/6–8 tbsp stale breadcrumbs or dried crumbs
sunflower oil, for frying
ground cinnamon, for dusting

FOR THE SAUCE
450g/1lb blackcurrants or blackberries
90g/31/2oz/1/2 cup sugar, plus extra for dusting

Directions

1 Put the milk, lemon rind, cinnamon stick and sugar in a pan and bring to the boil, stirring gently. Cover and leave to infuse for 20 minutes.
2 Put the cornflour and flour in a bowl and beat in the egg yolks with a wooden spoon. Add a little of the milk and beat to make a smooth batter.
3 Strain the remaining hot milk into the batter, then pour back into the pan. Cook over a low heat, stirring constantly. (The mixture won't curdle, but it will thicken unevenly if you let it.) Cook for a couple of minutes, until it thickens and separates from the side of the pan.
4 Beat the mixture hard with the spoon to ensure a really smooth consistency.Pour into an 18–20cm/7–8in, 1cm/1/2in-deep rectangular dish, and smooth the top. Cool, then chill until firm.
5 Make the fruit sauce. Cook the blackcurrants or blackberries with the sugar and a little water for about 10 minutes until soft.
6 Reserve 30–45ml/2–3 tbsp whole currants or berries, then put the rest in a food processor and blend to make a smooth purée. Return the purée and berries to the pan.
7 Cut the chilled custard into eight or twelve squares. Beat the eggs in a shallow dish and spread out the breadcrumbs on a plate. Lift half of the squares into the egg. Coat on both sides, then lift into the crumbs and cover all over. Repeat with the second batch of squares.

8 Pour about 1cm/1/2in oil into a deep frying pan and heat until very hot.

9 Lift two or three coated squares into the oil and fry for a couple of minutes, shaking or spooning the oil over the top, until golden. Reserve on kitchen paper, while frying the other batches.

10 To serve, arrange the custard squares on plates and sprinkle with sugar and cinnamon. Pour a circle of warm sauce round the squares, distributing the whole berries evenly.

COOK'S TIP

In Spain, milk is usually drunk at breakfast or used for cheese. In northern Spain, the milk has a wonderful quality and has been given special status as a dessert ingredient. Most popular of all the milk desserts are leche frita, flan and filloas (thin pancakes).

Nutritional information per portion: Energy 272kcal/1150kJ; Protein 7.7g; Carbohydrate 48.1g, of which sugars 27.1g; Fat 6.8g, of which saturates 2.7g; Cholesterol 146mg; Calcium 151mg; Fibre 2.2g; Sodium 169mg.

Apple-Stuffed Crêpes

Spain's dairy country lies along the cooler northern coast and crêpes are
extremely popular there. In the Asturias, crêpes are made with a variety of sweet fillings such as this apple one.

SERVES 4

115g/4oz/1 cup plain (all-purpose) flour
pinch of salt
2 large (US extra large) eggs
175ml/6fl oz/3/4 cup full-fat (whole) milk
120ml/4fl oz/1/2 cup sweet (hard) cider
butter, for frying
4 eating apples
60ml/4 tbsp caster (superfine) sugar
120ml/8 tbsp clear honey, and 150ml/1/4 pint/2/3 cup double (heavy)
cream, to serve

Directions

1 Make the batter. Sift the flour and salt into a large bowl. Add the eggs and milk and beat until smooth. Stir in the cider. Leave to stand for 30 minutes.
2 Heat a small heavy non-stick frying pan. Add a little butter and ladle in enough batter to coat the pan thinly. Cook the crêpe for about 1 minute until golden

underneath, then flip it over and cook the other side until golden. Slide the crêpe on to a plate, then repeat with the remaining batter to make seven more. Set the crêpes aside and keep warm.

3 Make the apple filling. Core the apples and cut them into thick slices. Heat 15g/1/2oz butter in a large frying pan. Add the apples to the pan and cook until golden on both sides. Transfer the slices to a bowl with a slotted spoon and sprinkle with sugar.

4 Fold each pancake in half, then fold in half again to form a cone. Fill each withsome of the fried apples. Place two filled pancakes on each dessert plate. Drizzle with a little honey and serve at once, accompanied by cream.

Nutritional information per portion: Energy 489kcal/2057kJ; Protein 8.2g; Carbohydrate 71.5g, of which sugars 49.6g; Fat 20.1g, of which saturates 11.3g; Cholesterol 139mg; Calcium 137mg; Fibre 2.1g; Sodium 69mg.

Torrijas

Translated as “poor knights”, these sugared toasts are perfect for almost every occasion. They make a good tea-time snack, or a delicious accompaniment to a cup of hot chocolate.

SERVES 4

120ml/4fl oz/1/2 cup white wine
12 thick rounds of stale French bread
2 large eggs
60–90ml/4–6 tbsp sunflower oil
ground cinnamon, and caster (superfine) sugar, for dusting

Directions

1 Pour the wine into a shallow dish and dip the bread rounds into it. Beat the eggs together in another shallow dish. Dip half the bread rounds into the beaten egg on each side so that they are completely covered.
2 Heat 60ml/4 tbsp oil in a pan until very hot and fry the bread rounds for about 1 minute on each side until crisp and golden. Reserve on kitchen paper, then dip and fry the rest, adding more oil if necessary. Serve hot, sprinkled with cinnamon and sugar.

COOK’S TIP

These toasts are often enjoyed at festivals and are a typical dish from Madrid. Milk can be used in place of white wine, if liked, making them suitable for children.

Nutritional information per portion: Energy 419kcal/1763kJ; Protein 12.2g; Carbohydrate 56.3g, of which sugars 3g; Fat 15.7g, of which saturates 2.4g; Cholesterol 95mg; Calcium 138mg; Fibre 2.4g; Sodium 652mg.

Churros

This Spanish breakfast doughnut is sold in all tapas bars, which so conveniently transform into cafés in the morning. They are also served at festivals, piped into great vats of oil, cut into loops and then tied with grass string to eat as you walk.

MAKES 12–15

200g/7oz/13/4 cups plain (all-purpose) flour
1.5ml/1/4 tsp salt
30ml/2 tbsp caster (superfine) sugar
250ml/8fl oz/1 cup water
60ml/4 tbsp olive or sunflower oil
1 egg, beaten
caster (superfine) sugar and ground cinnamon, for dusting
oil, for deep-frying

Directions

1 Sift the flour, salt and sugar on to a plate or piece of baking parchment. Put the water and oil in a pan and bring to the boil.

2 Tip the flour mixture into the pan and beat with a wooden spoon until the mixture forms a stiff paste. Leave to cool for 2 minutes, then gradually beat in the egg to make a smooth dough.

3 Oil a large baking sheet. Sprinkle plenty of sugar on to a plate and stir in a little cinnamon.

4 Spoon the dough into a large piping (pastry) bag fitted with a 1cm/1/2in plain piping nozzle.Pipe little coils or "S" shapes on to the baking sheet.

5 Heat 5cm/2in of oil in a large pan to 168°C/336°F, or until a little piece of dough dropped into the oil sizzles on the surface.

6 Using an oiled metal spatula, lower several of the piped shapes into the oil and fry for about 2 minutes until light golden.

7 Drain the churros on kitchen paper, then dip them into the sugar and cinnamonmixture, to coat. Cook the remaining churros in the same way and serve immediately.

Nutritional information per churro: Energy 111kcal/464kJ; Protein 1.7g; Carbohydrate 12.5g, of which sugars 2.3g; Fat 6.4g, of which saturates 0.9g; Cholesterol 13mg; Calcium 22mg; Fibre 0.4g; Sodium 5mg.

BiscochoBorracho

The name of this dessert translates as "drunken cake", indicating that it is soaked in brandy-flavoured syrup. This version of the recipe is made in a mould, then turned out.

SERVES 6–8

butter, for greasing
90g/31/2oz/3/4 cup plain (all-purpose) flour
6 large (US extra large) eggs
90g/31/2oz/1/2 cup caster (superfine) sugar
finely grated rind of 1 lemon
90ml/6 tbsp toasted flaked almonds
250ml/8fl oz/1 cup cream, to serve

FOR THE SYRUP
115g/4oz/1/2 cup caster (superfine) sugar
120ml/4fl oz/1/2 cup boiling water
105ml/7 tbsp Spanish brandy

Directions

1 Starting 1–2 days ahead, preheat the oven to 200°C/ 400°F/Gas 6. Butter a shallow pan, about 28 × 18cm/11 × 7in. Line the tin with baking parchment and butter well. Sift the flour a couple of times into a bowl. Separate the eggs, putting the whites into a bowl. Put the yolks in a food processor with the sugar and lemon

rind and beat until light. Whisk the whites to soft peaks, then work a little white into the yolk mixture.

2 Dribble two spoonfuls of the yolk mixture across the whites, sift some flour over the top and cut in gently with a large spoon. Fold together in this way until all the egg mixture and flour have been incorporated. Turn the cake mixture into the prepared shallow pan and smooth over. Bake for 12 minutes. Leave the cake to set for 5 minutes, then turn out on to a wire rack. Peel off the paper and leave to cool completely.

3 Make the syrup. Place 50g/2oz/1/4 cup sugar into a small pan and add 15ml/1 tbsp water. Heat until it caramelizes. As soon as it colours, dip the base of the pan into a bowl of cold water. Add the remaining sugar and pour in the boiling water. Bring back to a simmer, gently stirring until all the sugar has dissolved. Pour into a jug (pitcher) and add the brandy.

4 Put the cake back into the pan and drizzle half the syrup over it. Choose a 700ml/11/2 pint/3 cup capacity mould; cut the cake into scallops with a spoon and layer half into the bottom of it. Sprinkle 30ml/2 tbsp almonds over the top and into the cracks. Top with the remaining cake and nuts. Pour the remaining syrup over the cake, cover with foil and weight down the top. Chill until ready to serve. To serve, turn the cake out on to a dish, sprinkle with almonds and serve with the fresh cream.

Nutritional information per portion: Energy 412kcal/1719kJ; Protein 8.9g; Carbohydrate 37.1g, of which sugars 28.3g; Fat 23.2g, of which saturates 9.6g; Cholesterol 176mg; Calcium 96mg; Fibre 1.2g; Sodium 64mg.

Guirlache

This is an Arab sweetmeat from the Pyrenees, combining toasted nuts and caramel to produce a crisp nut brittle – a forerunner of some familiar chocolate bar fillings. It is less well known than turrón, the Spanish
Christmas nougat, which is made with similar ingredients.

MAKES ABOUT 24 PIECES

115g/4oz/1 cup almonds, half blanched, half unblanched
115g/4oz/1 cup hazelnuts, half blanched, half unblanched
5ml/1 tsp almond oil or a flavourless oil
200g/7oz/1 cup sugar
15ml/1 tbsp lemon juice

Directions

1 Preheat the oven to 150°C/300°F/Gas 2. Sprinkle the nuts on a baking sheet and toast for 30 minutes, shaking the sheet occasionally. The nuts should smell pleasant and have turned brown and be very dry.
2 Coarsely chop the toasted nuts or crush them roughly with a rolling pin. Cover another baking tray with foil and grease it with the oil.

3 Put the sugar in a pile in a small pan and pour the lemon juice round it. Cook over a high heat, shaking the pan, until the sugar turns a coffee colour. (As it cooks, the pile of sugar will melt and collapse into caramel.)

4 Immediately tip in the nuts and stir once, then pour the mixture on to the foil and spread out into a thin, even layer. Leave the mixture to harden.

5 Once set, break up the caramel into pieces and store in an airtight tin.

Nutritional information per piece: Energy 94kcal/395kJ; Protein 1.7g; Carbohydrate 9.3g, of which sugars 9.1g; Fat 5.8g, of which saturates 0.5g; Cholesterol 0mg; Calcium 23mg; Fibre 0.7g; Sodium 1mg.

Panellets

The Catalan name for these nutty festival cakes means "little bread", but they are, in fact, closer to marzipan, with a slightly soft centre that is produced by their secret ingredient – sweet potato. They are made for All Saints' Day, on 1st November, when families take flowers to the graveyards.

MAKES ABOUT 24

115g/4oz sweet potato, diced
butter, for greasing
1 large (US extra large) egg, separated
225g/8oz/2 cups ground almonds
200g/7oz/1 cup caster (superfine) sugar, plus extra for sprinkling
finely grated rind of 1 small lemon
7.5ml/11/2 tsp vanilla extract
60ml/4 tbsp pine nuts
60ml/4 tbsp pistachio nuts, chopped

Directions

1 Cook the sweet potato in a pan of boiling water for 15 minutes, or until soft. Drain and leave to cool.
2 Preheat the oven to 200°C/400°F/Gas 6. Line one or two baking sheets with foil and grease well with butter.
3 Put the sweet potato in a food processor and process to a smooth purée (paste). Work in the egg yolk,

almonds, sugar, lemon rind and vanilla extract to make a soft dough. Transfer the dough to a bowl and chill for 30 minutes.

4 Spoon walnut-sized balls of dough on to the foil, spacing them about
2.5cm/1in apart, then flatten them out slightly. Lightly beat the egg white in a bowl and brush over the cakes. Sprinkle half the cakes with pine nuts, about5ml/1 tsp each, and half with pistachio nuts. Sprinkle with sugar and bake for 10minutes, or until lightly browned.

5 Leave to cool on the foil, then lift off and store in an airtight container.

Nutritional information per cake: Energy 130kcal/541kJ; Protein 3.1g; Carbohydrate 10.7g, of which sugars 9.6g; Fat 8.6g, of which saturates 0.8g; Cholesterol 8mg; Calcium 32mg; Fibre 1g; Sodium 20mg.

Pestiños

The Arabs invented all sorts of sweet bites, to eat after the main course or with drinks. Bathed in honey syrup, pestiños were often deep-fried and known as dulces de sárten, which means "sweets from the frying pan". However, you can bake them and they puff beautifully in the oven.

MAKES ABOUT 30

225g/8oz/2 cups plain (all-purpose) flour, plus extra for dusting
60ml/4 tbsp sunflower oil
15ml/1 tbsp aniseed, lightly crushed
45ml/3 tbsp caster (superfine) sugar
250ml/8fl oz/1 cup water
60ml/4 tbsp anisette
3 small (US medium) eggs

FOR THE ANIS SYRUP
60ml/4 tbsp clear honey
60ml/4 tbsp anisette or Ricard

Directions

1 Preheat the oven to 190°C/375°F/Gas 5. Sift the flour on to a sheet of baking parchment. Heat the oil in a small pan with the crushed aniseed, until the aniseed releases its aroma. Strain the oil into a larger pan and

add the sugar, water and anisette. Heat to a rolling boil.

2 Remove the pan from the heat and add the sifted flour, all in one go. Beat vigorously with a wooden spoon until the mixture leaves the sides of the pan clean. Leave to cool.

3 Meanwhile lightly beat the eggs. Gradually incorporate the egg into the dough mixture, beating hard. You may not need to use all the egg; the paste should be soft but not sloppy. Reserve any remaining beaten egg.

4 Grease and flour two baking sheets. Fit a plain nozzle to a piping (pastry) bagand pipe small rounds of dough about 2.5cm/1in across on the sheets, spacingthem about 2cm.1in apart. Brush with the remaining beaten egg. Bake for about 30 minutes, or until lightly brown and an even texture right through. (Lift one off the sheet to test.)

5 Melt the honey in a small pan and stir in the anisette. Just before serving, use a slotted spoon to dunk the pestiños into the syrup.

Nutritional information per bun: Energy 65kcal/272kJ; Protein 1.3g; Carbohydrate 8.9g, of which sugars 3.2g; Fat 2.1g, of which saturates 0.3g; Cholesterol 19mg; Calcium 14mg; Fibre 0.2g; Sodium 8mg.

Twelfth Night Bread

January 6th, Epiphany, celebrates the arrival of the kings at Christ's manger, and in Spain it is the day for exchanging Christmas gifts. This bread is specially baked for the occasion. Traditionally it contains a bean, a china baby or a coin, and the person to find it is declared king of the party.

SERVES 12

450g/1lb/4 cups unbleached strong white bread flour
2.5ml/1/2 tsp salt
25g/1oz fresh yeast
140ml/scant 1/4 pint/scant 2/3 cup mixed lukewarm milk and water
75g/3oz/6 tbsp butter
75g/3oz/6 tbsp caster (superfine) sugar
10ml/2 tsp finely grated lemon rind
10ml/2 tsp finely grated orange rind
2 eggs
15ml/1 tbsp brandy
15ml/1 tbsp orange flower water
silver coin or dried bean (optional)
1 egg white, lightly beaten, for glazing

FOR THE DECORATION
a mixture of glacé (candied) fruit slices
flaked (sliced) almonds

Directions

1 Lightly grease a large baking sheet. Sift together the flour and salt into a large bowl. Make a well in the centre.

2 In a bowl, mix the yeast with the milk and water until the yeast has dissolved. Pour into the centre of the flour and stir in enough of the flour from around the sides of the bowl to make a thick batter.

3 Sprinkle a little of the remaining flour over the top of the batter and leave to turn spongy, in a warm place, for about 15 minutes or until frothy.

4 Using an electric whisk or a wooden spoon, beat together the butter and sugar in a bowl until soft and creamy.

5 Add the citrus rinds, eggs, brandy and orange flower water to the flour mixture and mix to a sticky dough.

6 Beat the mixture until it forms a fairly smooth dough. Gradually beat in the butter mixture and beat for a few minutes until the dough is smooth and elastic. Cover with lightly oiled clear film (plastic wrap) and leave to rise, in a warm place, for about 11/2 hours, or until doubled in size.

7 Punch the dough down and turn out on to a lightly floured surface. Gently knead for 2 or 3 minutes, incorporating the lucky coin or bean, if using.

8 Using a rolling pin, roll out the dough into a long strip measuring about 65 × 13cm/26 × 5in.

9 Roll up the dough from one long side like a Swiss roll (jelly roll) to make a long sausage shape. Place seam side down on the prepared baking sheet and seal the ends together. Cover with lightly oiled clear film and leave to rise, in a warm place, for 1–11/2 hours, or until doubled in size.

10 Preheat the oven to 180°C/350°F/Gas 4. Brush the dough ring with lightly beaten egg white and decorate with glacé fruit slices, pushing them slightly into the dough. Sprinkle with flaked almonds and bake for 30–35 minutes, or until risen and golden. Turn out on to a wire rack to cool.

Nutritional information per portion: Energy 217kcal/914kJ; Protein 4.8g; Carbohydrate 36g, of which sugars 7.4g; Fat 6.7g, of which saturates 3.7g; Cholesterol 45mg; Calcium 69mg; Fibre 1.2g; Sodium 54mg.

Pan De Cebada

Galicia is known for its country breads, which often include flours other than wheat. A combination of barley and maize flours gives this bread a close, heavy texture and a rich taste.

MAKES 1 LARGE LOAF

cornmeal, for dusting

FOR THE SOURDOUGH STARTER
175g/6oz/11/2 cups cornmeal
225g/8oz/2 cups strong wholemeal (whole-wheat) bread flour
75g/3oz/2/3 cup barley flour

FOR THE DOUGH
20g/3/4oz fresh yeast
45ml/3 tbsp lukewarm water
225g/8oz/2 cups strong wholemeal bread flour
15ml/1 tbsp salt

Directions

1 Make the starter. In a pan, mix thc cornmeal with 300ml/1/2 pint/11/4 cups water, then blend in another 300ml/1/2 pint/11/4 cups of water. Cook over a gentle heat, stirring, until thickened. Transfer to a large bowl and cool.

2 Put the mixture into a food processor. Work in the wholemeal and barley flours and process thoroughly. Return the starter to the bowl, cover with clear film (plastic wrap) and leave in a warm place for 36 hours.

3 To make the dough, put the yeast and water in a small bowl and cream together. Return the sourdough starter to the food processor, pour in the yeast mixture and process to combine well. Gradually add the wholemeal flour, with the salt, and work the whole dough until it becomes smooth and elastic. Transferthe dough to a lightly oiled bowl, cover with clear film and leave, in a warmplace, for 11/2–2 hours until nearly doubled in size.

4 Return the dough to the food processor and use the pulse button to work it to a smooth dough. Dust a baking sheet with cornmeal, and shape the dough on it to a plump round. Sprinkle with a little cornmeal. Cover with a large upturned bowl. Leave to rise, in a warm place, for about 1 hour, or until nearly doubled in size.

5 Preheat the oven to 220°C/425°F/Gas 7 and place a roasting pan in the bottom of the oven. Pour 300ml/1/2 pint/11/4 cups cold water into the roasting pan. Lift the bowl off the risen loaf and put the baking sheet in the oven. Bake the bread for 10 minutes. Remove the pan of water, reduce the oven temperature

to 190°C/375°F/Gas 5 and bake for about 20 minutes. Cool on a wire rack.

Nutritional information per loaf: Energy 2265kcal/9588kJ; Protein 81.5g; Carbohydrate 463.5g, of which sugars 10.8g; Fat 17.3g, of which saturates 1.4g; Cholesterol 0mg; Calcium 214mg; Fibre 55.5g; Sodium 17mg.

CPSIA information can be obtained
at www.ICGtesting.com
Printed in the USA
LVHW011233070121
675556LV00002B/117

9 781914 192210